Forward

Traditional concepts defining most corporate bond investments are often relatively straightforward with respect to the underlying portfolio strategies commonly used to achieve wealth and success in the financial markets. Intelligent income investors understand that companies issue corporate bonds as a way to raise cash without the dilution of ownership that comes with new stock issues. Corporate bonds are also senior to stock, so principle and interest must be paid to bondholders before dividends are paid to stockholders. In these ways (and many others), corporate bonds help establish important advantages for investors that are looking to design an approach to portfolio strategy that is both innovative and secure over long-term time horizons.

At the same time, portfolio strategists will often miss the wide variety of ways insider trading activity can work as an excellent indicator of corporate credit quality and strength in these areas should always be viewed as a prerequisite for investors with a goal to achieve high levels of current income. Additionally, investors can reduce sensitivity to changes in market interest rates by selecting short durations bonds issued by companies with a fortress balance sheet. When viewed in conjunction with publicly available insider trading information, quantitative screening techniques can be used to help investors identify companies that are extraordinarily well-capitalized as potential selections to be included as part of a multi-faceted portfolio strategy.

In this guide to insider income investing, we explain why the major credit ratings agencies fail investors and fall behind the curve in their assessments of corporate credit quality. In this book, the first chapter will help to set initial parameters for investors that are defining an investment strategy based on short duration bond portfolios. Chapter 2 covers the basic factors used by major ratings agencies when determining corporate credit ratings. In Chapter 3, important lessons from the 2008 financial crises are discussed in order to a provide an informative historical context and to better understand the vulnerable framework which characterizes modern credit ratings systems.

In Chapter 4, we build on this framework and outline strategies proactive investors can use to avoid the risks that are commonly encountered in the market's bond benchmarks. Chapter 5 covers recent macroeconomic challenges that have emerged within the current bond market environment. Chapters 6-7 show investors how to identify critical mischaracterizations in corporate credit ratings, using recent examples in the market performances of Twitter and General Electric. In Chapter 8, we discuss some of the ways income investment strategies can benefit from trends in insider trading as they relate to the broader direction of the market.

In Chapter 9, we discuss ways insider buying or selling activities can work as momentum indicators. These trends are further evaluated in Chapter 10, which includes historical backtesting data for insider trading strategies that have been shown to consistently outperform the S&P 500 as a benchmark. In Chapter 11, we discuss some of the challenges that are often encountered by investment strategies that use traditional valuation metrics in isolation.

In Chapter 12, we outline ways investors can combine income investment strategies and reach optimal gains over long-term time horizons. Chapter 13 offers methods for investors to overcome recent challenges in corporate bond markets. Finally, Chapter 14 discusses foundational strategies to structure income portfolios for long-term success. Using the combined approach to income investing outlined in this guide, we hope portfolio managers will be able to identify new strategies that capture high levels of current income with limited sensitivity to unpredictable changes in market interest rates.

- APEX RESEARCH

Insider Income Investment Guide

Table of Contents

Chapter 1:

Defining an Investment Strategy: Short Duration Bond Portfolios

Chapter 2:

Corporate Credit Ratings: Basic Factors

Chapter 3:

Important Lessons for Investors: 2008 Financial Crisis

Chapter 4:

Proactive Strategies to Avoid Risks in Common Bond Benchmarks

Chapter 5:

Emerging Macro Challenges in Current Market Environments

Chapters 6-7:

Identifying Mischaracterizations in Credit Ratings: General Electric

Identifying Mischaracterizations in Credit Ratings: Twitter

Chapter 8:

Income Strategies: Insider Trading and Broader Market Direction

Chapter 9:

Insider Buying/Selling Actions as Momentum Indicators

Chapter 10:

Historical Backtesting: Insider Trading Strategies Consistently Outperform S&P 500 Benchmark

Chapter 11:

Problems Using Traditional Valuation Metrics in Isolation

Chapter 12:

Combining Income Investment Strategies

Chapter 13:

Overcoming Current Challenges in Corporate Bond Markets

Chapter 14:

Long-Term Strategies to Structure Income Portfolios

Investment Strategy: Short Duration Bond Portfolios

Investors seeking to capture high levels of current income with low sensitivity to changes in market interest rates can accomplish these goals by investing in short-term bonds issued by companies with an above-average level of insider buying activity. Utilizing publicly available insider trading information filed with the Securities and Exchange Commission (SEC), quantitative screening techniques can be used to help investors identify companies that are extraordinarily well-capitalized (more current assets than total liabilities) as potential selections to be included as part of a multi-faceted portfolio strategy.

When focusing on bond investments with an average effective maturity of less than four years and an average credit rating of BBB (or higher), portfolio strategists can monitor trading decisions by corporate insiders as potential buy/sell signals. In many cases, these insider trading signals will be contrarian in nature. As a result, this innovative approach to bond portfolio construction can create unique opportunities for investors to generate enhanced returns and outperform results that are commonly seen in the broader market.

In this guide to insider income investing, we will see that the major credit ratings agencies typically fall behind the curve in their assessments of corporate credit quality and individual investors are often unaware of important company-specific events likely to influence the future outlook. Using the multi-faceted approach to income investing outlined in this guide, portfolio strategists will be able to identify new ways to capture high levels of current income with limited sensitivity to unpredictable changes in market interest rates.

Important elements noted in this portfolio investment approach will include:

- **Insider-Driven Strategies:** Invest in short-term corporate bonds offered by companies whose top-level managers are buying shares of their own stock. Corporate insiders (directors, CFOs, CEOs, etc.) understand their own firm better than any outsider possibly could. Thus, their actions have a strong positive correlation with future asset performances.

- **Limited Credit Risks:** Companies with rising levels of insider buying tend to experience bankruptcies and loan defaults at substantially lower rates. It stands to reason that corporate insiders wouldn't be willing to initiate a sizable equity stake if their company is in jeopardy of bankruptcy.

- **Reduced Sensitivity to Interest Rates:** Corporate bond portfolios (average credit quality of BBB or higher) can reduce exposure to interest rate risks with an average modified duration of less than three years. This approach offers income investors added protection when macro environments are characterized by uncertain changes in market interest rates.

Intuitive concept: Why wouldn't investors first look at insider buying as a way to evaluate corporate credit quality?

In simple terms, insider investment strategies seek to capitalize on buying and selling signals generated by the actions of market insiders. These are the people with the closest relationship to the organization, its board, its management team, and the company-specific factors that are most likely to impact credit quality metrics in the future.

Since primary insiders have informational advantages that go above and beyond what is available to the average investor, historical research shows that tremendous returns can be achieved when investors follow their decisions. Essentially, heavy insider activity (cluster buying or selling) can be a tremendous filter for credit quality and this information can help investors generate superior returns when compared to the recommendations made by popular credit ratings agencies that typically assess corporate bonds.

Unfortunately, the stark reality is that companies are often misrated by Standard & Poor's, Moody's, and Fitch. Well-known examples include the investment-grade credit ratings that were given to companies like AIG, Bear Sterns, and Lehman Brothers during the lead-up to the 2008 financial crisis. Most of the current evidence suggests that the major ratings agencies have done very little to correct the errors of their ways in the periods that followed. As a result of these important factors, it's clear that investors shouldn't rely on these organizations as a way of gauging the true quality of corporate bond investments.

As we will see in the following historical case studies, businesses are much more likely to exhibit superior credit quality if insiders are buying company stock in ways that represent an extreme divergence from the long-term transactional averages. At the same time, there are only a few investment funds (globally and in the U.S.) that track insider buying/selling decisions and enable "average" investors to benefit from strategies that are based on the actions of corporate insiders. This creates a substantial need for innovative bond funds that are designed to capitalize on the valuable information contained in the decisions of high-level corporate insiders.

In most cases, the upper-management team at any organization is in the best position to identify market situations that are most favorable for their company. Furthermore, top-level corporate insiders aren't likely to be buying their own company's stock right before the company defaults on its debt. As a result, credit assessments made by top corporate insiders often carry a predictive value that surpasses the ratings given by the three major agencies.

Since these credit ratings tend to be followed by a majority of the investment community, inevitable divergences between perception and reality can create sizable contrarian investment opportunities for anyone seeking sustainable portfolio income. As we will see from the examples discussed in this investment guide, increased levels of insider activity often lend additional internal credibility to strategies utilizing a combined approach that draws from each of these portfolio elements. For these reasons, income investors can benefit from shorter-term bond durations while focusing on companies that exhibit heavy insider buying activity by their top executives.

Investor Summary –

Keys to Success and Elements to Avoid:

Given all the challenges that face income investors in the current market environment, investors should consider the following keys to success when making asset selections for an income portfolio:

- Locate firms with a fortress balance sheet that is validated by a strong outlook in its underlying debt/equity metrics.
- Focus on bonds with short maturities to avoid the uncertainties that are experienced during unpredictable interest rate environments.
- Identify compelling buy/sell trigger signals that are based on trading decisions made by top-level corporate insiders.
- During recent market periods characterized by rising interest rates, most bond funds struggled. Looking at the aggregate bond index, market trends show that many of these bond funds are structured around maturities above seven years.
- Generally, funds that have managed to outperform implement strategies based on bond durations that are far shorter than those seen in the typical bond fund.
- When focusing on an average maturity of less than three years, investors are not hit with the same negative influences seen during market periods characterized by rising interest rates.

In the following guide to insider income investing, we will discuss the wide variety of risks typically associated with longer duration bond funds that follow recommendations made available by the major credit ratings agencies. As we will see in the following examples, historical backtesting data show that insider strategies based on a combined approach to portfolio investment have the potential to create significant advantages for proactive income investors.

Historical Context: Should Investors Trust Ratings Agencies?

(Negative examples highlighting risks from the 2008 financial crisis help explain why traditional bond analysis that relies solely on the opinions of credit rating agencies can be misleading for income investors)

Corporate Credit Ratings: Basic Factors

Corporate credit ratings give investors access to the opinions of each major agency with respect to the performance outlook of a firm and the likelihood that its businesses will be able to meet the future requirements of its financial obligations. Ideally, the corporate credit rating given to a company will provide a clear indication of its ability (on a relative basis) to repay its creditors.

For investors, this analysis provides additional information which can be used to price the yields associated with a company's debt securities. However, it must be understood that corporate credit ratings are not facts —they're merely opinions. In many cases, there will be significant disagreements amongst the major ratings agencies themselves, despite having all of the same data points (publicly available statistics) from which to base their decisions.

Common Credit Rating Characterizations

Standard & Poor's, Fitch, and Moody's are the most popular agencies that provide corporate credit ratings to the market. Each of these agencies uses its own ratings system and the following table shows their various ratings characterizations (outlined with accompanying explanations):

Credit Rating Scales by Agency, Long-Term

Moody's	S&P	Fitch		
Aaa	AAA	AAA	Prime	
Aa1	AA+	AA+	High grade	
Aa2	AA	AA		
Aa3	AA-	AA-		
A1	A+	A+	Upper medium grade	
A2	A	A		
A3	A-	A-		
Baa1	BBB+	BBB+	Lower medium grade	
Baa2	BBB	BBB		
Baa3	BBB-	BBB-		
Ba1	BB+	BB+	Non-investment grade speculative	"Junk"
Ba2	BB	BB		
Ba3	BB-	BB-		
B1	B+	B+	Highly speculative	
B2	B	B		
B3	B-	B-		
Caa1	CCC+	CCC	Substantial risk	
Caa2	CCC		Extremely speculative	
Caa3	CCC-		Default imminent with little prospect for recovery	
Ca	CC	CC		
	C	C		
C	D	D	In default	
/				
/				

(Graphic Source: Wolf Street)

Here, we can see that the basic terminology used by the three major credit ratings agencies is somewhat different. However, similarities exist in that these classifications are designed to make distinctions between companies that are below investment grade (speculative or "junk" status) and companies that are viewed as having superior credit quality.

Of course, even the most stellar corporate credit ratings won't guarantee that a company can actually repay all of its future debt obligations. This is why investors often find it useful to view corporate credit ratings on a more relative basis. Overall, these ratings have a long-term track record which outlines differences in the general level of creditworthiness that is visible amongst rated companies. Studies conducted by Standard & Poor's have found that investment-grade corporate bond issuers have a five-year average default rate of 1.07%. In contrast, the Standard & Poor's studies found that speculative-grade companies (holding "junk" status) have a five-year average default rate of 16.03%.

Reliability of Corporate Credit Ratings

During the periods that led to the 2008 financial crisis, many firms sporting investment-grade credit ratings from the three major agencies began to exhibit signs of financial weakness. However, many companies that held investment-grade ratings would later be downgraded to junk status. For many investors, the eventual quickness (and ultimate severity) of these downgrades called into question the reliability of the agencies ratings themselves.

Central concerns revolve around the fact that clear biases influence the decisions made by the major ratings agencies. Critics argue that before the job to conduct corporate credit rating can be secured, there is likely to be an implied agreement between the agency and the client company to produce a favorable report which neglects to mention negative factors that might downwardly impact ratings characterizations. In the aftermath of the 2008 financial collapse, investors called for intensive public scrutiny which ultimately revealed critical flaws in the market's credit rating systems.

Remembering the Past Highlights Potential Future Risks

Due to obvious historical tendencies that suggest the presence of ratings bias, investors must consider the overall credibility of the three major agencies when constructing income portfolio strategies.

To place these assessments within the proper historical context, it makes sense for income investors to remember the lessons that were learned during the 2008 financial crisis:

- Six days before the collapse of Lehman Brothers, ratings agency Standard & Poor's maintained its A-level credit rating on the company.
- Moody's held Lehman's investment-grade rating even longer, waiting until one business day prior to the company's market-shattering bankruptcy before making its downgrade.
- American International Group (AIG) had an investment-grade A-rating from Standard & Poor's less than one week prior to nationalization.
- Bear Stearns and Merrill Lynch had investment-grade credit ratings as they were being rescued by J.P. Morgan and Bank of America.
- Freddie Mac and Fannie Mae had AAA ratings when forced into conservatorship.

- **Conclusion:** Major ratings agencies always seem to be the last to know.

Important Lessons for Investors: 2008 Financial Crisis

When constructing an income portfolio, investment strategists must understand that the collective performances shown by the major ratings agencies on the eve of the economic collapse of 2008 revealed systematic weaknesses and significant conflicts of interest that have not been corrected more than a decade later.

Perhaps the most memorable example can be found in Lehman Brothers, which filed for bankruptcy on Sept. 15, 2008 with $619 billion in debt and $639 billion in assets.

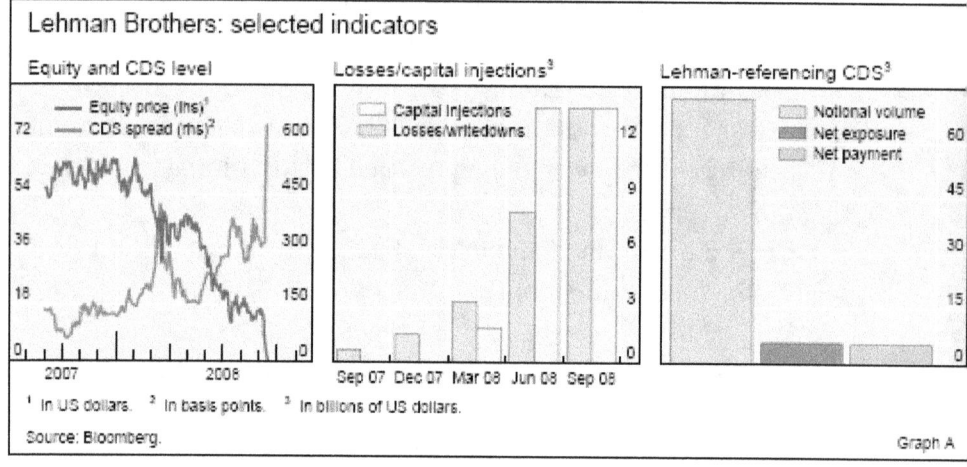

(Source: Bloomberg)

Six days before the collapse of Lehman Brothers, ratings agency Standard & Poor's maintained its A-level credit rating on the company. Moody's held Lehman's investment-grade rating even longer, waiting until one business day prior to the company's market-shattering bankruptcy before making its downgrade. Lehman's assets far surpassed those of Enron and WorldCom, which made their bankruptcy filings the largest in history. However, these are just a few of many costly examples that impacted investors.

Overall, the financial crisis cost people living in the United States roughly $12.8 trillion and these events forever changed the way investors secure their assets. Unfortunately, the ratings mischaracterizations discussed in the following sections demonstrate continued systemic weakness remain present in the market's commonly accepted ratings procedures.

2008 Financial Crisis: Long-Term Impact

In the chart timeline shown below, we can see that American International Group (NYSE: AIG) had an investment-grade A-rating from Standard & Poor's less than one week prior to nationalization:

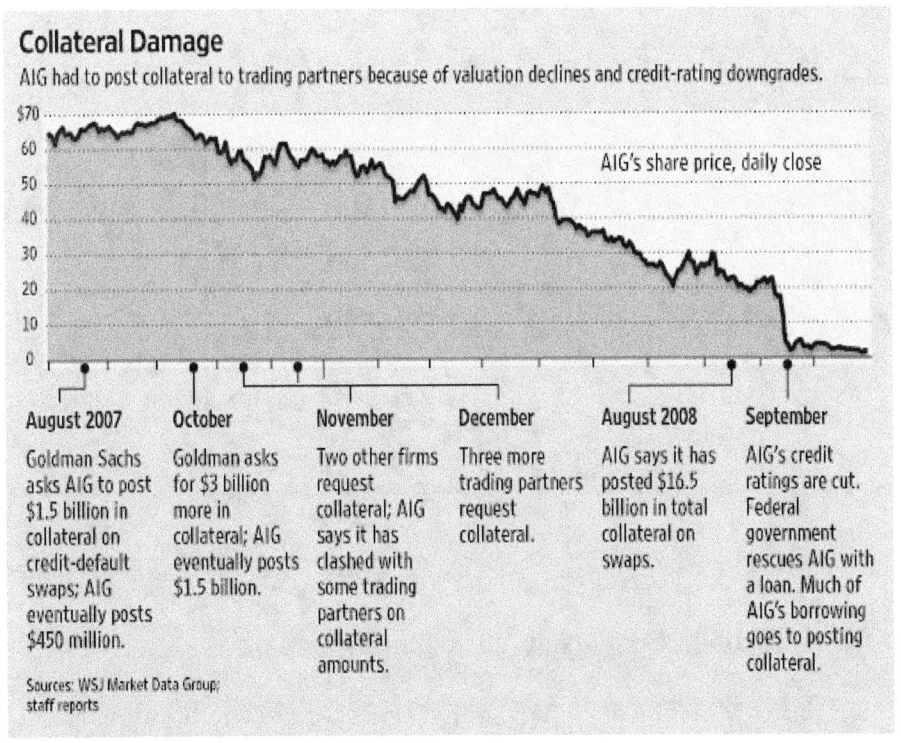

(Source: Wall Street Journal)

In the next example, we can see that an elevated credit rating help propel shares of Bear Stearns stock to record levels just 15 months before the company needed a bailout to avoid total collapse.

On January 12th, 2007, Bear Stearns stock closed at all-time highs of $171.51 per share. By the beginning of 2008, the stock had lost more than half of its value as investors began to question the sustainability of the company's balance sheet metrics. Surprisingly, Bear Stearns still had an investment-grade credit rating as the company was being rescued by J.P. Morgan:

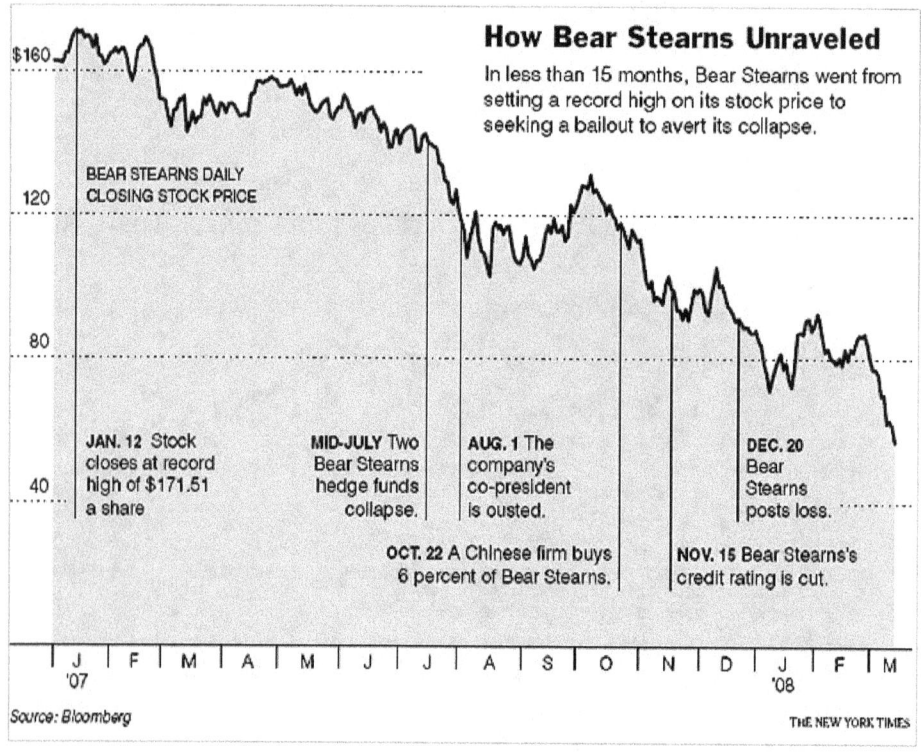

(Source: Bloomberg / New York Times)

Similarly, Merrill Lynch had an investment-grade credit rating as the company was being rescued by Bank of America. This occurred even while Merrill Lynch displayed clear weaknesses in its 2007 full-year performances from continuing operations.

Full Year Results of Operations					
	2007	2006	2005	2004	2003
	(DOLLARS IN MILLIONS)				
Total Revenues	62,675	69,352	46,848	31,916	27,392
Less Interest Expense	(51,425)	(35,571)	(21,571)	(10,416)	(7,844)
Revenues, Net of Interest Expense	11,250	33,781	25,277	21,500	19,548
Non-Interest Expenses	24,081	23,971	18,516	15,992	14,474
Pre-Tax (Loss)/Earnings from Continuing Operations	(12,831)	9,810	6,761	5,508	5,074
Income Tax (Benefit)/Expense	(4,194)	2,713	1,946	1,244	1,341
Net (Loss)/Earnings from Continuing Operations	(8,637)	7,097	4,815	4,264	3,733
Pre-Tax Earnings from Discontinued Operations	1,397	616	470	327	146
Income Tax Expense	537	214	169	155	43
Net Earnings from Discontinued Operations	860	402	301	172	103
Net (Loss)/Earnings Applicable to Common Stockholders	(8,047)	7,311	5,046	4,395	3,797

(Source: Company Filings)

Obvious problems in Merrill Lynch's mortgage businesses led to massive write-offs in 2007, which were completely ignored by the major credit ratings agencies:

Merrill's Mortgage Business by The Numbers					
	2007	2006	2005	2004	2003
	(DOLLARS IN MILLIONS)				
Cash Flows From Securitizing Residential Mortgage Loans	100,219	95,883	58,002	N/A	N/A
Mortgages, Mortgage-backed, and Asset-backed Trading Assets	28,013	44,401	29,233	26,877	8,382
Loans, Notes, and Mortgages (Net of Allowances) on Balance Sheet	94,992	73,029	66,041	53,262	12,427

Reflects Massive Write-offs

(Source: Company Filings)

Even more concerning, Freddie Mac and Fannie Mae had AAA ratings when forced into conservatorship in 2008 (despite a major crash in full-year net income for 2007):

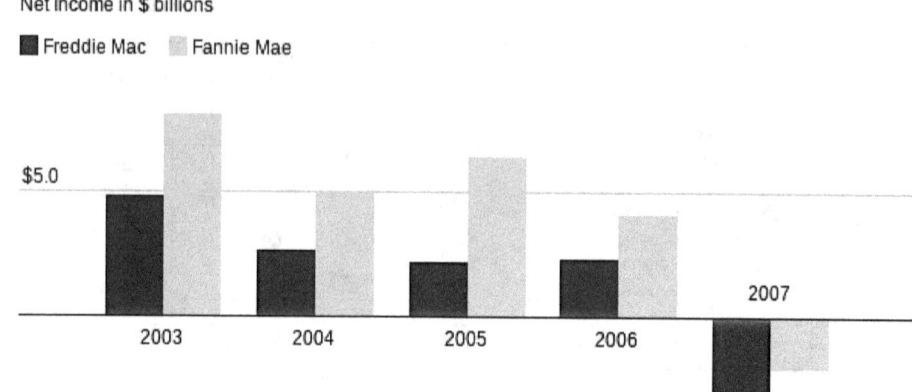

(Source: Freddie Mac / Fannie Mae Annual Reports)

Of course, this is a terrible track record of ratings mischaracterizations (across several different industries) and the bulk of the evidence shows that inaccuracies from the major agencies continue to put investors at risk. Broadly speaking, a total of 83% of the securities that were rated AAA by the three major ratings agencies in 2006 received a credit downgrade within the next four years.

Tragically, these credit downgrades brought a substantial amount of collateral damage to anybody with pre-crisis exposure to related assets and many Americans lost substantial portions of their retirement savings.

How Did Ratings Agencies Explain the Problem?

Essentially, the major agencies made the argument that their credit ratings are simply opinions (which are protected by the First Amendment). However, this explanation does nothing to resolve the losses weathered by income investors that lost money based on the inaccuracy of their recommendations. Following the crisis, a general lack of accountability and structural reform allowed all three of the major ratings agencies to effectively ignore the impending collapse of MF Global in 2011:

(Source: Bankruptcy Data / SEC Filings)

Even though the major credit ratings agencies were under heavy scrutiny (both from the general public and from the U.S. government), Fitch and Moody's didn't remove MF Global's investment-grade rating until just six days before the company filed for bankruptcy protection. Even worse, Standard & Poor's waited until the day of the bankruptcy filing before downgrading the defunct broker.

Lack of Systemic Reform Shows Things Haven't Changed

Over time, these types of errors show that the major credit rating agencies have done little to change the clear flaws in their methodology. More than likely, this is because no significant legislative changes have been made in order to ensure the ratings agencies improve on the integrity of their actions.

(Source: SEC / Economist.com)

As a result, income investors remain vulnerable when portfolio strategies rely solely on recommendations that are tainted by a clear conflict of interest. Another problem is that no meaningful effort was put in place to increase competition within the industry in the years that followed the 2008 financial crisis. During this period, the market share of Moody's, Standard & Poor's, and Fitch remained largely unchanged.

Standard & Poor's and Moody's continue to hold a near duopoly in the industry (dominating roughly 80% of its market share), even with clear examples of repeated failure showing that their inaccurate ratings systems have put investors at risk. In other words, the most influential conspirators in the financial market meltdown of 2008 have maintained their prominent positions in the industry, despite a seemingly constant public outcry for reform in the years that followed these events.

After the financial crisis, an in-depth investigation was conducted by the Securities and Exchange Commission to identify systemic weaknesses within the ratings industry. The findings indicated significant conflicts of interest with rated companies, an intentional unwillingness to communicate with investors when changes were made in ratings models, and a general lack of consistency in the ratings formulas used to analyze corporate credit quality. Many academics and industry analysts still consider these trends to be a problem, suggesting that the statistical models used to rate credit quality are both esoteric and outdated.

In fact, the U.S. Congress has even gone so far as to ban the major ratings agencies from participating in the processes used to determine capital requirements for banks. Thus, it's clear that the Securities and Exchange Commission has deep legislative concerns about the reliability of the ratings industry. Since the 2008 financial crisis, the SEC's annual reports show that there's no evidence which suggests the industry's careless underwriting standards and practices of routine misbehavior have changed in a meaningful way.

Income Investors: Continued Risks Require Proactive Strategies

Needless to say, all of this creates monumental risks for income investors. Essentially, this is the reason the SEC levied a $58 million penalty against Standard & Poor's in 2015 while citing a list of nefarious activities in its accepted ratings processes. In the report, the SEC explained that S&P "elevated its own financial interests above investors by loosening its rating criteria to obtain business and then obscuring these changes from investors."

Furthermore, the Financial Crisis Inquiry Report found that companies will frequently tell the ratings agencies that they will go to a competitor if an unfavorable credit rating is given to the business. In other words, if Moody's gives a negative corporate bond rating after making its initial assessments, the company in question can simply take their business to Fitch or Standard & Poor's to get a better result.

Since the major ratings agencies are paid by the companies they rate, they have a profit incentive to be undiscerning and this is why most corporate bond investments continue to be tainted by obvious conflicts of interest. As an analogy, this would be similar to college students paying their professors for the grades they give in class. As things currently stand, the corporate bond market's ratings model creates massive incentives for the three major agencies to alter their standards whenever it's convenient (in an effort to gain more business).

Unfortunately, the minor monetary fines that have been levied in recent years have done little to change these flaws in the system. Since publicly traded companies are able to pay for a favorable rating, income investors should not view this information as reliable when constructing a portfolio strategy. Even today, it's clear that the market is in desperate need of a new model that increases competition within the industry and allows credit raters to work more directly for investors.

Absent these structural changes in the system, proactive income investors should instead look to insider trading activities as a preferred indicator of corporate credit quality. When used in conjunction with common sense balance sheet analysis, insider trading strategies make it easier for income investors to isolate and identify the best corporate bond investments available in the market.

Emerging Macro Challenges in Current Market Environments

In addition to these conflicts of interest that continue to plague the corporate credit ratings industry, investors have seen significant macroeconomic challenges develop in recent years. Specifically, average duration levels in the aggregate bond index have increased while yields have fallen:

(Source: Barclays)

As interest rate uncertainties continue to grow, these challenging macroeconomic trends help to explain why many bond funds have experienced difficulties in recent years. In 2018, many bond funds were flat (or down), yet it's clear that a well-positioned minority of the market's available bond fund selections managed to outperform.

Why? How can investors avoid risks and position their investments during uncertain periods characterized by changing interest rate levels?

―――――

Proactive Strategies to Avoid Risks in Common Bond Benchmarks

- Since the end of the financial crisis, the Bloomberg Barclays U.S. Aggregate Bond Index has seen a sharp rise in its average duration (reaching its highest levels on record).
- At the same time, the Bloomberg Barclays U.S. Aggregate Bond Index has seen a decline in average credit ratings.
- As a result, investors could be vulnerable to increased credit risks and/or interest rate risks when selecting portfolio components that blindly track a benchmark bond index.
- When designing a strongly positioned corporate bond fund, investors must pay strict attention to its duration intervals and the underlying credit quality contained in its asset exposure.

Many investors rely on exchange-traded funds (ETFs) or mutual funds which track a commonly watched bond index as a strategic approach to fixed-income portfolio investment. Unfortunately, investors often find that a chosen income portfolio strategy will contain much more risk than initially anticipated. As a result, it is critical to assess the credit quality of the fund's underlying holdings in order to ensure each component matches required investing horizons and specific risk tolerance levels.

Recent changes in the broader bond market have eliminated many of the benefits typically associated with investment strategies that use an index-based approach to fixed income portfolio construction. In the following sections, we will look at some of the reasons which explain why this has come to be the case.

Rising Bond Durations

Typically, income investors will use the Bloomberg Barclays U.S. Aggregate Bond Index as an important strategic benchmark and the rising popularity of these assets can be visualized in the massive increase in market value we've seen over the last four decades:

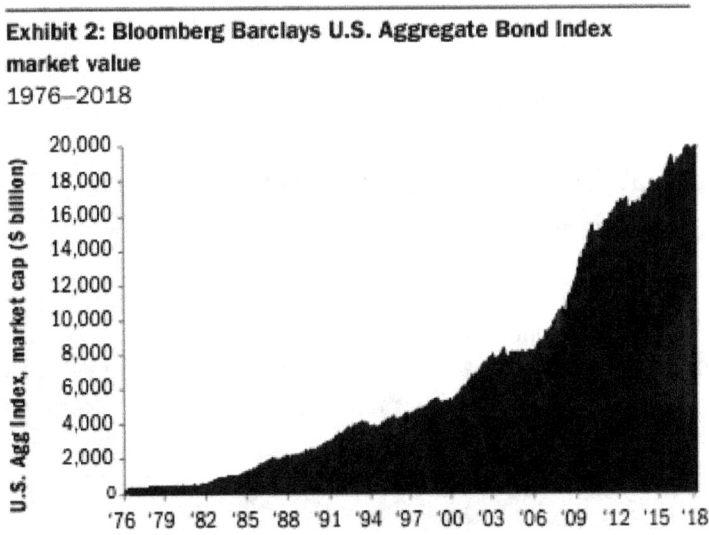

Exhibit 2: Bloomberg Barclays U.S. Aggregate Bond Index market value 1976–2018

Source: Bloomberg, data as of 07/31/18.

(Source: Bloomberg)

In the past few years, however, changes in the composition of the Bloomberg Barclays U.S. Aggregate Bond Index have been characterized by an increase in the average duration (which eventually swelled to record levels).

For investors, these trends are critically important because changes in the average bond duration can create additional vulnerabilities when bond prices are negatively impacted by unpredictable fluctuations in the market's underlying interest rate levels.

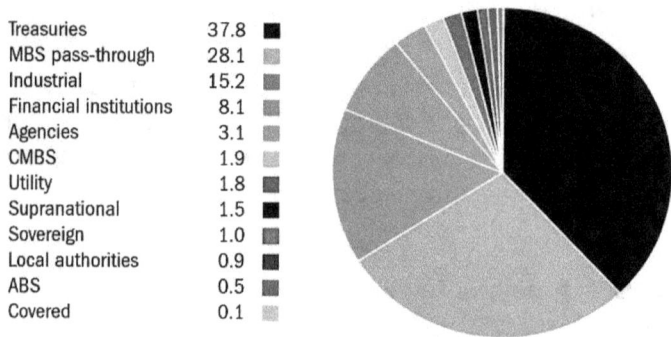

Bloomberg Barclays U.S. Aggregate Bond Index, sector breakdown (%)

Sector	%
Treasuries	37.8
MBS pass-through	28.1
Industrial	15.2
Financial institutions	8.1
Agencies	3.1
CMBS	1.9
Utility	1.8
Supranational	1.5
Sovereign	1.0
Local authorities	0.9
ABS	0.5
Covered	0.1

(Source: Bloomberg)

Historical Context: Average Durations in the Aggregate Bond Index

From 1989 to 2008, the average duration in the Bloomberg Barclays U.S. Aggregate Bond Index was just 4.5 years. Since the 2008 financial crisis, however, the average duration levels present within the aggregate bond index have risen sharply:

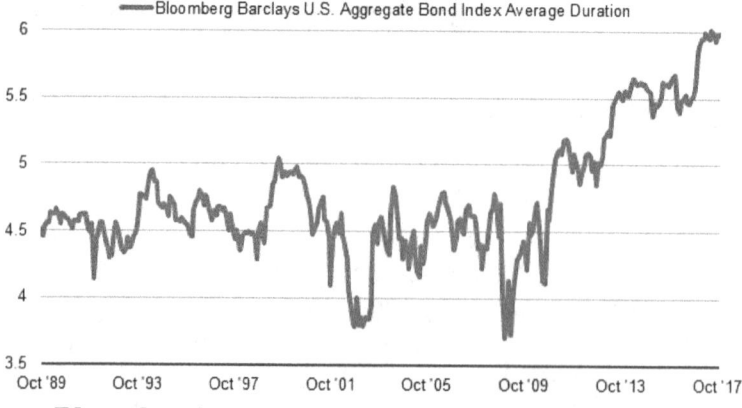

(Source: Bloomberg)

In the previous chart, we can see that the average bond duration is currently holding well above those figures. But recent trend changes in the bond market have actually forced the long-term average higher, rising to 4.8 years. As a result, it's clear that we have moved into market regions that tend to be much more sensitive to unexpected changes in interest rates:

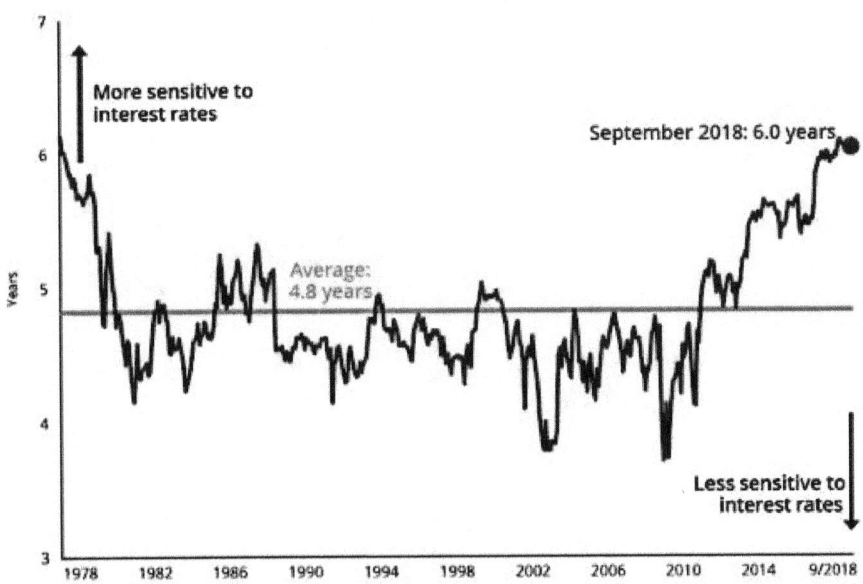

(Source: Bloomberg)

Thus, it's undeniable that the market is in the process of developing trends that indicate significant deviations away from the historical averages. Since these changes have drifted in directions that are almost entirely disruptive (with respect to traditional bond portfolio strategies), it's important for income investors to develop an approach to investing that is uniquely effective, multi-faceted, and consistently capable of providing protection from unnecessary losses during unpredictable market environments.

What specific effects can higher durations have on corporate bond prices?

Everything else being equal, rising durations can make corporate bond prices more sensitive to macro changes in interest rates. Unfortunately, these influences can have a dramatic impact on the returns generated by popular bond funds. With most corporate bond investments exposed to elevated durations (as high as 7-9 years in many cases), it's clear that added risks have become visible for income investors.

This helps to explain why so many of the market's favorite corporate bond funds underperformed and disappointed investors in 2018. By extension, income investments with substantial exposure to recent trend effects in the Bloomberg Barclays U.S. Aggregate Bond Index may have implicitly accepted deeper interest rate sensitivity and an increase in self-imposed risk tolerance. In many cases, this has occurred without even making significant changes to the underlying components of the investment portfolio.

Characteristics of Recent Trends in Corporate Bond Markets

Specifically, the average duration levels seen in the corporate bond market are clearly elevated in relation to other areas of the bond market:

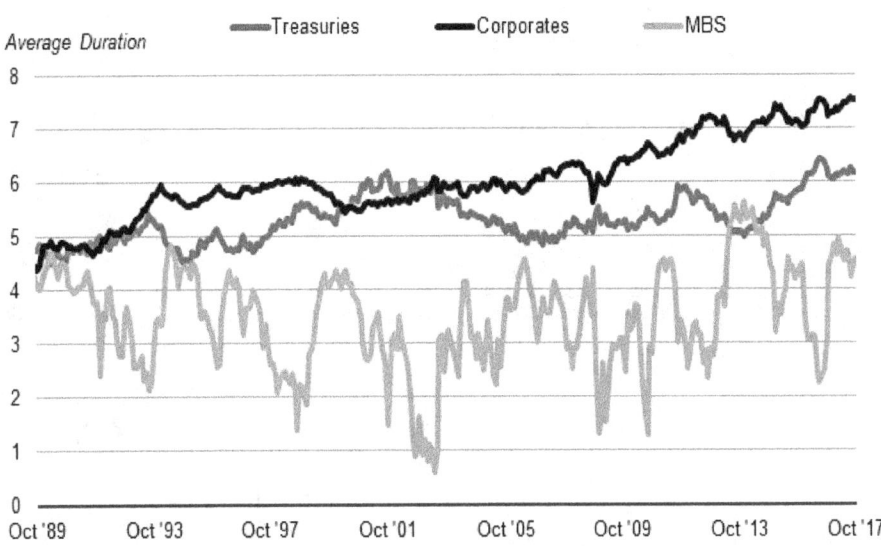

(Source: Bloomberg)

When it comes to the topic of average bond duration levels, a simple rule of thumb for investors is that the price of a bond (or bond fund) will increase or decrease by 1% per annual period of duration for each modification of 1% in the interest rate level for similar maturities. In other words, if the average duration of the aggregate index is six years, a bond fund that is based on the performance of that index would consequently see prices fall by about 6% in cases where interest rates increase by one percentage point. In historical terms, this decline is much more substantial when compared to what these types of bond funds have experienced in the past.

What Caused These Challenging Trends to Develop?

Rising value changes in the average duration of the Bloomberg Barclays U.S. Aggregate Bond Index resulted after corporations took advantage of historically low long-term interest rates (following the 2008 financial crisis) and issued larger amounts of corporate debt in the periods that followed. Ultimately, an increase in the duration of most corporate bond components disproportionately affected the index while its averages moved above the seven-year mark.

During the same period, the average duration of the Bloomberg Barclays U.S. Treasury Bond Index has not experienced trend changes that are quite as extreme. However, the index has moved high enough to reach levels that are near the upper end of the statistical range that has developed over the last three decades. Durations in mortgage-backed securities are also above their long-term averages, so these are upward trends that have been fairly consistent throughout the market as a whole.

Macro Vulnerabilities: Declines in Corporate Credit Quality

In addition to the rising challenges created by broader trends in interest rates, investors also face risks associated with declining corporate credit quality in the underlying assets of many bond funds. If we look at the average credit quality in the Bloomberg Barclays U.S. Aggregate Bond Index, levels can be somewhat misleading because U.S. Treasuries make up nearly 40% of its composition.

However, the cross-section of securities with corporate credit ratings at the lower end of the spectrum (amongst investment-grade assets) has been growing steadily over time. Some interesting conclusions can be drawn when we look at the period which immediately preceded the 2008 financial crisis. In 2007, bonds with single-A and triple-B ratings made up just 16% of the Bloomberg Barclays U.S. Aggregate Bond Index.

In the decade that followed, this cross-section of lower-rated bonds rose steadily (to reach 25%):

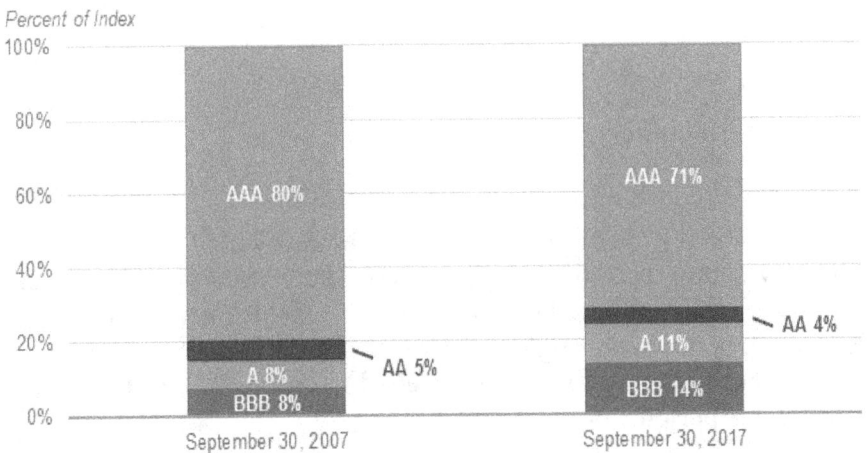

(Source: Bloomberg)

Throughout the market, many of these declining trends were driven by changes in the average credit ratings of corporate bonds. Not surprisingly, the Bloomberg Barclays U.S. Corporate Bond Index saw its average credit rating drop significantly in the period that followed the financial crisis. Essentially, this is because the cross-section of lower-rated bonds on the corporate index increased significantly during this period:

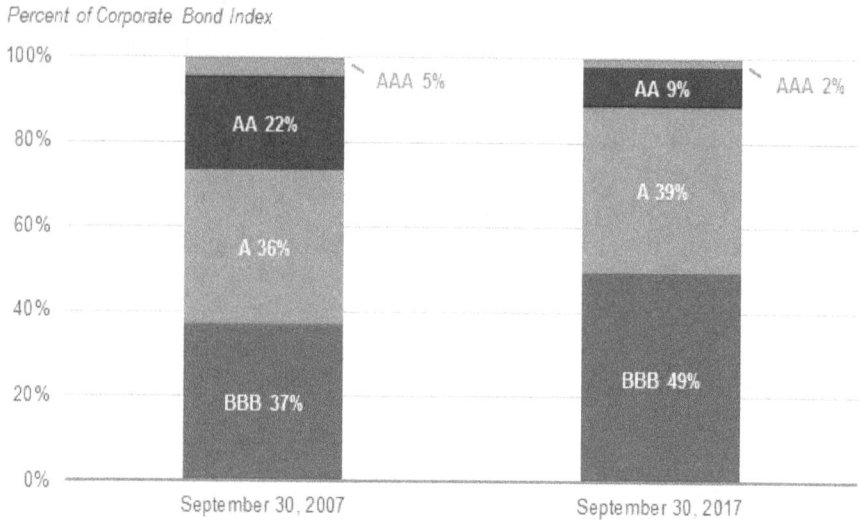

(Source: Bloomberg)

In 2007, about 27% of the Bloomberg Barclays U.S. Corporate Bond Index was composed of highly rated corporate issuers. By 2017, this figure had fallen to just 11%. Put another way, the number of corporate bonds with single-A and triple-B ratings (the lowest investment-grade credit ratings) swelled to **reach 88% of the index** during this period.

In practical terms, this means that investments in index funds that track the corporate bond market could result in increased exposure to corporate bonds with a credit rating that is below an investor's accepted risk threshold. The reality is that not all corporate bonds with investment-grade credit ratings are created equal and investors must use common sense from a balance sheet analysis perspective when assessing the potential strength or weakness of each corporate bond component that's present in any income investment portfolio.

Outperforming in Deteriorating Credit Environments

When used in conjunction with changes in insider buying activity and short-term bond durations, historical data show that this multi-faceted approach can raise the potential for enhanced returns in fixed-income investing. Companies that possess a strong balance sheet and the added support of insider buying activity are less likely to default on future debt obligations.

Focusing on each of these factors can aid in the construction of a combined analysis approach which allows income investors to avoid excessive credit risk in an increasingly challenging market environment. In the following sections, we will look at some of the ways income investors can develop a successful and effective process for selecting asset components within a bond investment portfolio.

Developing Strategies to Overcome Ratings Agency Risks

- Ratings agencies continue to inaccurately assess corporate outlook / credit quality despite the well-documented failures that became apparent after the 2008 financial crisis.
- Misguided characterizations from the major ratings agencies and unpredictable changes in market interest rate levels may continue to create challenges for investors.
- Income investors must use time-tested strategies when assessing the potential strength or weakness of any corporate bond investment.
- Buy/Sell signals generated by insiders and common sense from a balance sheet analysis perspective are the best methods for assessing credit quality.

In the following historical examples, we will look at several important metrics that can be used to assess long-term changes in the credit outlook at four companies: General Electric, Twitter, Square, and J.P. Morgan Chase. When compared to the corporate credit ratings made publicly available by the major agencies, the metrics discussed below will indicate significant mischaracterizations in the relevant credit ratings made available by Standard & Poor's, Moody's, and Fitch. Fortunately, there are alternative strategies that are capable of working as viable solutions in spite of these ongoing challenges in the market.

Specifically, it should be understood that common sense from a balance sheet analysis perspective remains the best method for assessing long-term corporate credit quality. Ultimately, income investors could have identified emerging trends and spotted ratings mischaracterizations at each of these four companies through buy/sell signals generated by the investment decisions of top corporate insiders.

Fundamental Strategies: Assessing Balance Sheet Strength

When defining an approach to analyze a company's balance sheet, one of the most important metrics to consider is the Debt to Equity Ratio (D/E). Also referred to as the "debt-equity ratio", "gearing ratio", or "risk ratio", the D/E ratio is a leverage calculation that weighs a company's total debt liability against its shareholder equity.

In simple terms, the D/E ratio measures the degree to which companies finance their operations with debt (as opposed to wholly owned corporate funds and retained earnings). This figure allows investors to assess a company's ability to use shareholder equity and cover its financial obligations to creditors in the event of an unexpected downturn in the business.

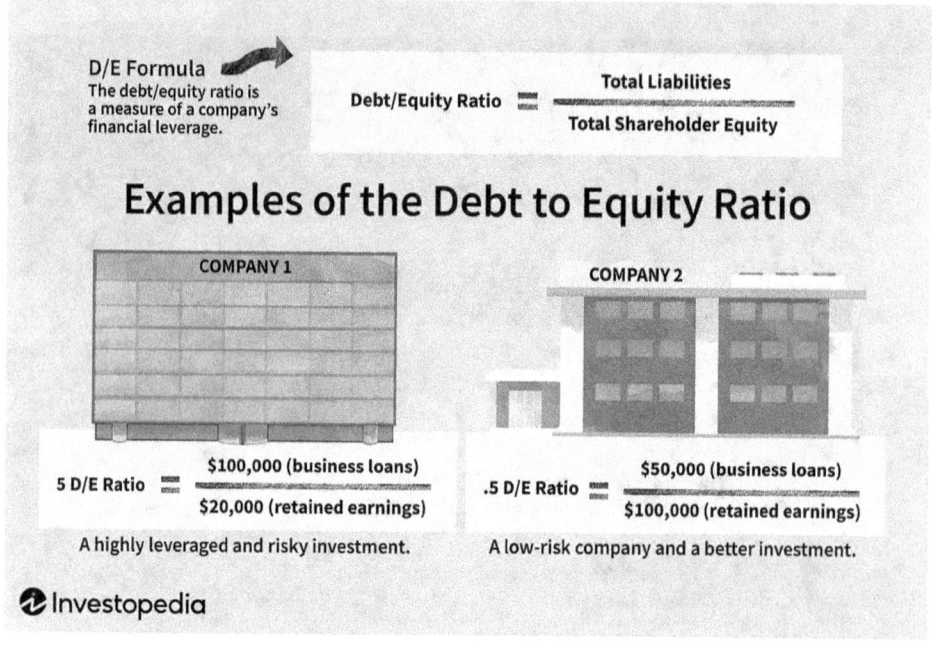

(Graphic Source: Investopedia)

Essentially, the short formula used to calculate the D/E ratio measures a company's total debt level relative to shareholder equity, unlike the Debt to Assets (D/A) ratio which puts the total assets figure in the denominator.

The long version of the D/E formula adds time variables to the equation and gives portfolio strategists a better idea of how the ratio defines the extent to which a company's shareholder equity is capable of fulfilling its debt obligations to creditors:

Debt to Equity Ratio = (Short-Term Debt + Long-Term Debt + Fixed-Payment Liabilities) / Shareholder Equity

The previous equation represents the long version of D/E formula and each of these additional figures can be found on the balance sheet of a firm's financial statements. All corporate balance sheets are required to show that total shareholder equity equals a company's assets after liabilities. As a result, the traditional balance sheet equation appears as the following:

Assets = Shareholder Equity + Liabilities

A firm's total debt level is determined by the sum of its short-term debt, long-term debt, and other obligations with fixed payment structures (i.e. capital leases) incurred under the normal operating cycles of its business. Debt schedules are created to separate liabilities into individual components, however, not all current (or non-current) liabilities will be considered debt. Below, we can see examples of several balance sheet items that may or may not be considered debt:

What is considered debt?

- *Bonds payable*
- *Capital lease liabilities*
- *Drawn lines of credit*
- *Long-term debt obligations*
- *Current portion of long-term debt*
- *Notes payable*

What isn't considered debt?

- *Dividends payable*
- *Accounts payable*
- *Deferred revenues*
- *Accrued expenses*

Various categories contained on a company's balance sheet might show individual accounts that aren't normally considered "equity" or "debt" in the way a loan or book value might be considered when analyzing the credit quality of an asset. In other words, the D/E ratio can be distorted by factors like pension plan adjustments, intangible assets, or retained losses. However, the D/E ratio remains vital when investors are looking to analyze and identify companies that possess strong credit quality metrics that are sufficient for inclusion within a corporate bond investment portfolio.

Sample Calculations: Debt to Equity Ratio

Below is a visual example of the balance sheet calculations commonly used to determine the Debt to Equity Ratio of a business:

D/E Ratio Example

Short Term Debt:		
Notes Payable	$	26,000
Current Portion of Long Term Debt	$	30,000
Long Term Debt:		
Bond Payable	$	84,000
Other Fixed Payments	$	23,000
Total Debt	$	**163,000**
Shareholder's Equity	$	**37,000**
D/E Ratio		**4.41x**

(Graphic Source: Corporate Finance Institute)

In this hypothetical example, short-term debts include notes payable and current portions of long-term debt. The short-term figure is added to the long-term figure, which includes bonds payable and other fixed payments. The sum of total debt is $163,000, which is divided by shareholder equity of $37,000. This calculation gives us a final D/E ratio of 4.41x.

Advanced Techniques: D/E Ratio Modifications

Due to the ambiguities present for some accounts in primary categories of a company's balance sheet, income investors and portfolio strategists can modify the D/E ratio by including growth expectations, profit performances, and short-term leverage ratios in its calculations. Shareholder equity figures on a balance sheet are equal to the total value of a company's assets after accounting for liabilities. However, this is not the same as saying shareholder equity is fully represented when calculating a company's assets and subtracting the debt that's connected to those assets.

To resolve these differences, portfolio strategists can modify the D/E ratio in ways that are reflective of credit quality trends seen on longer-term time horizons. As part of the investment approach used in bond portfolio construction, short-term debt should still be included when assessing corporate leverage levels. But since these obligations should be paid within a one-year period, short-term debt shouldn't be viewed as the equivalent of long-term debt because it doesn't carry the same level of risk.

For example, let's assume that one company's balance sheet shows $3 million in shareholder equity, short-term payables (notes, accounts payable, wages, etc.) of $2 million, and long-term debt of $1 million. Now assume that another company's balance sheet shows $3 million in shareholder equity, short-term payables of $1 million and long-term debt of $2 million. In both cases, each company will have $3 million in shareholder equity. This means that the D/E ratio associated with both companies will be 1.00x.

At first glance, this seems to imply that the risk from the leverage held by both companies is identical. However, in reality, the amount of leverage and the total debt held by the second company is far riskier for those considering investments in corporate bonds. Long-term debt tends to be more expensive than short-term debt and it is more sensitive to unpredictable changes in market interest rates. As a result, the second company's cost of capital and expenses from interest will be higher. If interest rates drop in the future, it is likely that long-term debt will be refinanced. Intuitively, it might seem that increases in interest rates would favor companies holding larger amounts of long-term debt. But if bondholders can make redemptions on the debt, it can still create significant disadvantages for the company.

Income Investor's Strategy Summary - Key Points:

- Debt is often helpful to a company in cases where it can be used to facilitate expansion.
- However, when a company funds its operations with excessive amounts of borrowed money, the risk of bankruptcy can increase dramatically in the event of a downturn in the business.
- Proportions of debt and equity used by a company to finance operations can be expressed through D/E ratios, which ultimately signal the extent to which shareholder equity can fulfill the company's debt obligations.

Debt to Equity Ratio in Practice

As shown in the previous examples, a D/E ratio equal to 1.00x would imply investors and creditors find themselves on equal footing. However, if a company's balance sheet shows total debt of $100 million and total equity of $200 million, the company's D/E ratio would be 0.50x. In practical terms, this means the company has 50 cents in leverage for every dollar it has in equity. D/E ratios below 1.00x indicate lower levels of debt financing in relation to equity funding from shareholders.

Higher D/E ratios show that a company receives most of its financing through borrowed funds and this puts the company at greater risk if debt levels become insurmountable. Even if a business hasn't produced enough profit to meet its financial obligations, minimum debt payments must be paid when they become due. This is why sustained declines in quarterly earnings often lead to bankruptcy (or other forms of financial distress) whenever a company's D/E ratio shows excessive leverage is present on its balance sheet.

In simple terms, a business becomes more vulnerable to the possibility of bankruptcy when most of its operations are funded by borrowed capital. In contrast, companies with a D/E ratio below 1.00x are less levered and tend to have a lower risk of bankruptcy. However, the appropriate D/E ratio will also vary by industry. Thus, it's important to take a relative reading amongst a company's peer group in order to determine whether a company is likely to experience elevated debt risks.

Elevated D/E ratios indicate levered businesses and they should be viewed as significant warning signals for investors whenever a company's earnings outlook is in decline. For this reason, high D/E ratios are only favorable in companies with stable cash flow generation. In these cases, an elevated D/E ratio can be beneficial if stable cash flow allows a business to service debt obligations and increase equity returns using leverage.

Various Effects on Equity Return Metrics

In the following example, we will see how an increase in debt can be used to raise a company's equity returns. When a company makes a conscious decision to use debt (rather than equity) as a primary funding source, its balance sheet will show a smaller equity account. As a result, it becomes easier to show favorable values in the company's return on equity (ROE) figure and this may be viewed as preferable for certain approaches to portfolio investment strategy:

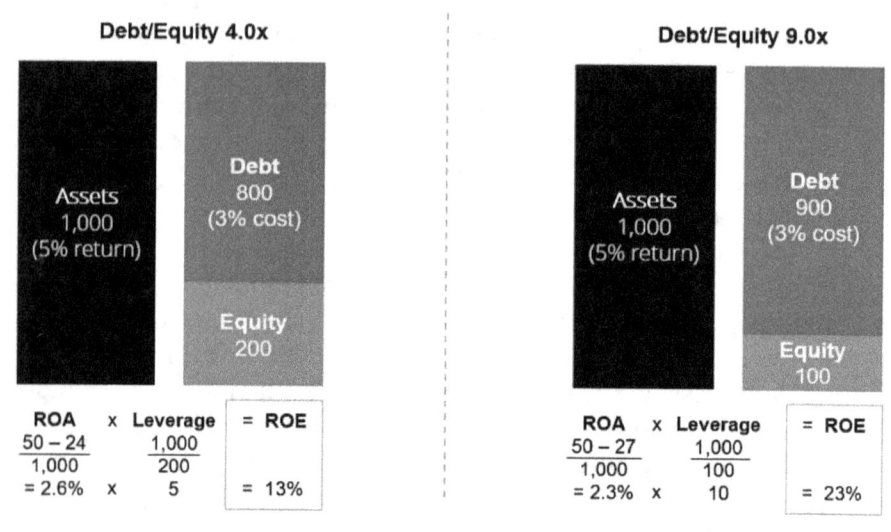

(Source: Corporate Finance Institute)

In the example above, we can see that raising the company's debt figure from 800 to 900 results in a D/E ratio that increases from 4.0x to 9.0x. However, similar reductions in the company's equity figure propels its ROE metric from 13% to 23%. Another benefit of this type of modification is that the cost of debt is typically lower relative to the cost of equity.

As a result, raising a company's D/E ratio can have the effect of lowering its weighted average cost of capital (WACC). However, significant negatives become apparent when a company's D/E ratio reaches extreme levels. As this occurs, losses on the company's balance sheet are compounded down and the firm may find itself in a position where it's no longer able to service its financial obligations. When a company's D/E ratio is too high, its borrowing costs will generally skyrocket (along with its cost of equity). As the WACC for the business rises, the effect on share prices is often negative.

Debt Metrics: Real-Time Comparisons

We can now apply these debt analysis techniques to real-time examples in the market as a way of comparing the relative strength of corporate bond investments. To accomplish this, we can compare the debt metrics of companies within the same peer group as well as those in different industry sectors.

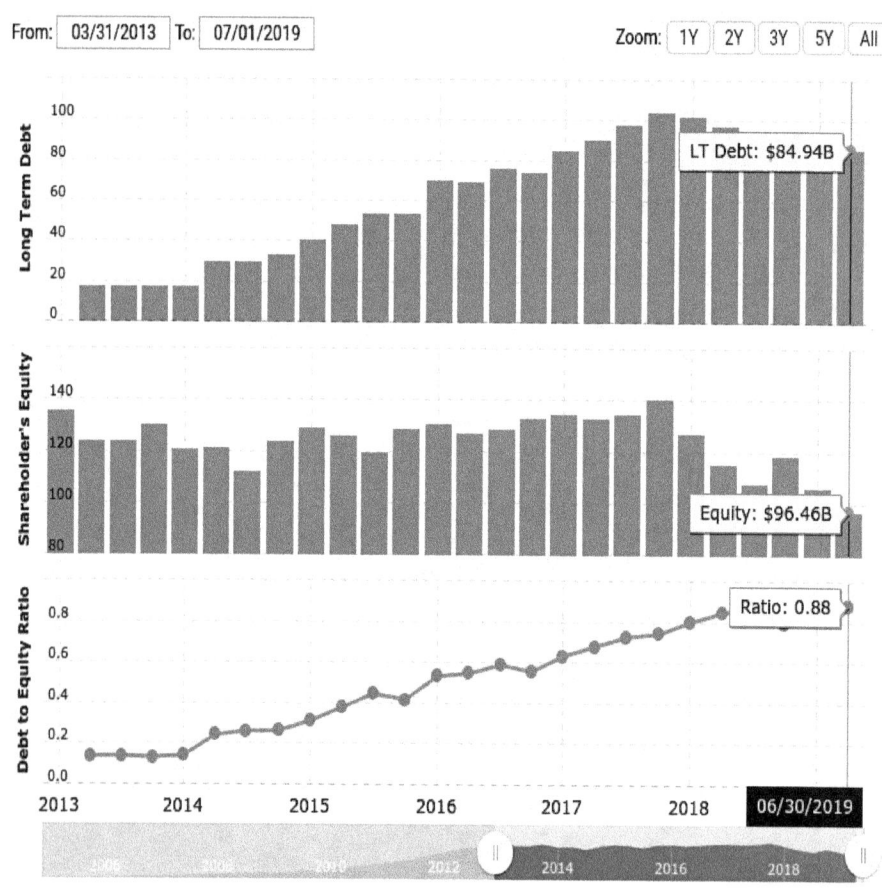

(Source: Macrotrends)

In the chart above, we can see below that Apple (NASDAQ:AAPL) had $84.94 billion in long-term debt and $96.46 billion in shareholder equity during the market period ending on 6/30/2019.

Apple's Debt to Equity Ratio for the period ending on 6/30/2019 can be calculated as: $84,940,000,000 ÷ $96,460,000,000 = 0.88. Essentially, this means Apple's balance sheet figures for the first half-year period of 2019 show that Apple had $0.88 in debt for every dollar of equity. Viewed in isolation, Apple's debt ratios provide investors with limited information, but income portfolio strategists can get a better sense of a company's debt ratios by comparing against the industry's averages.

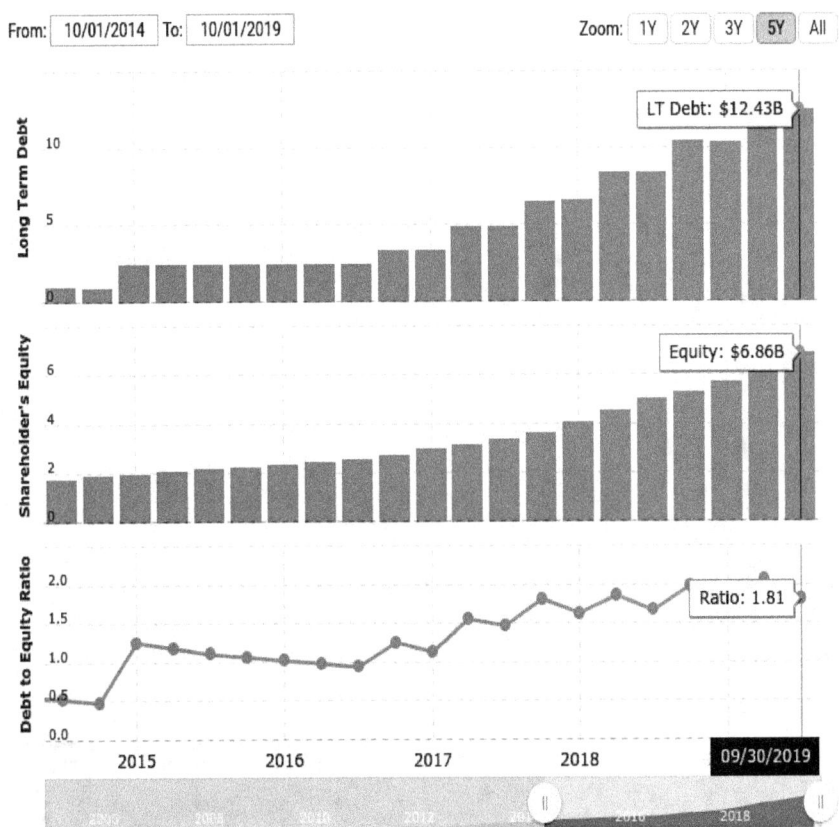

(Source: Macrotrends)

Another well-known tech company that operates in the streaming media sector is Netflix (NASDAQ:NFLX). For the period ending on 6/30/2019, the chart above shows that Netflix had $12.43 billion in long-term debt and $6.86 billion in shareholder equity.

Netflix's Debt to Equity Ratio for the period ending on 6/30/2019 can be calculated as: $12,430,000,000 \div \$6,860,000,000 = 1.81$. Results for the first half-year period of 2019 show Netflix had \$1.81 in debt for every dollar of equity. This debt ratio more than doubles the figure visible on Apple's balance sheet over the same period. Of course, this might lead some investors to perceive Apple as the superior investment (on a comparative basis). However, additional comparisons suggest that companies with an even better credit profile may be available to investors.

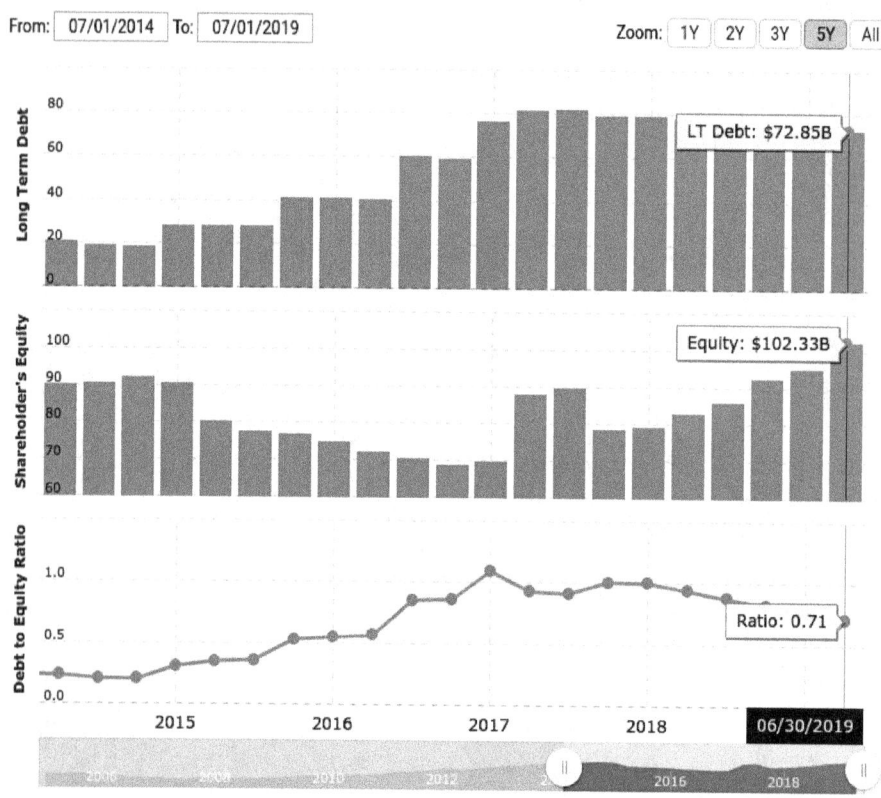

(Source: Macrotrends)

For the period ending on 6/30/2019, Microsoft Corp. (NASDAQ:MSFT) had \$72.85 billion in long-term debt and \$102.33 billion in shareholder equity. Microsoft's Debt to Equity Ratio for the period ending on 6/30/2019 can be calculated as: $72,850,000,000 \div \$102,330,000,000 = 0.71$.

Results for the first half-year period of 2019 show Microsoft had $0.71 in debt for every dollar of equity. This is below the debt ratio on Apple's balance sheet, and it gives investors a better sense of the market average for large-cap stocks in the tech sector.

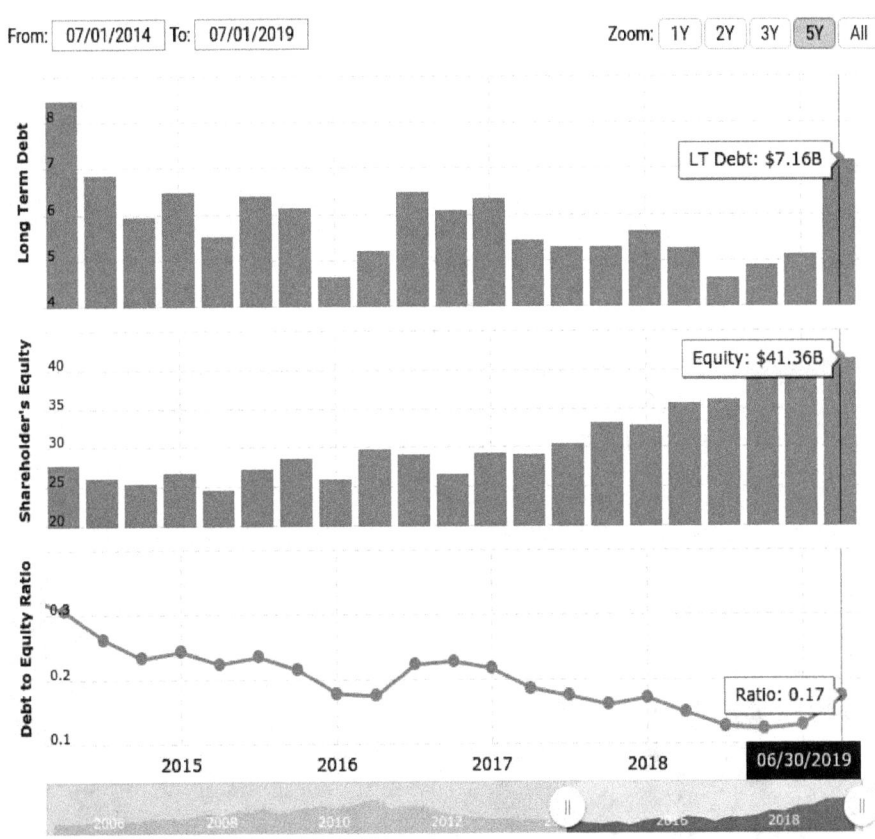

(Source: Macrotrends)

Finally, we will look at Sony Corp. (NYSE:SNE) had $7.16 billion in long-term debt and $41.36 billion in shareholder equity for the market period ending on 6/30/2019. Sony's Debt to Equity Ratio for the period ending on 6/30/2019 can be calculated as: $7,160,000,000 ÷ $41,360,000,000 = 0.17. Results for the first half-year period of 2019 show Sony had $0.17 in debt for every dollar of equity and this figure is far below the debt metrics visible on the balance sheets of Netflix, Apple, and Microsoft.

Relative Debt Ratios:

Selected tech companies in the period ending on 6/30/2019:

- **Apple, Inc.** (NASDAQ:AAPL) = 0.88x
- **Netflix, Inc.** (NASDAQ:NFLX) = 1.81x
- **Microsoft Corp.** (NASDAQ:MSFT) = 0.71x
- **Sony Corp.** (NYSE:SNE) = 0.17x

Overall, a comparison of the debt ratios of companies within their industries can offer a clear representation of the relative credit quality of each firm. Our first comparison of the credit profiles at Apple and Netflix may have inspired a preference for AAPL amongst investors. However, a deeper comparison of large-cap firms throughout the tech industry revealed two additional companies with debt metrics that were even more secure.

As we can see in the following chart, Apple's credit profile exposes investors to much higher debt levels when compared to Sony. Furthermore, these two companies have developed diverging trends in credit quality for the better part of five years. For income investors, this type of information can be valuable when analyzing potential selections that will be included in a corporate bond portfolio. As we will see in the extensive examples discussed in the following sections, credit ratings made by the three major agencies often neglect this important information.

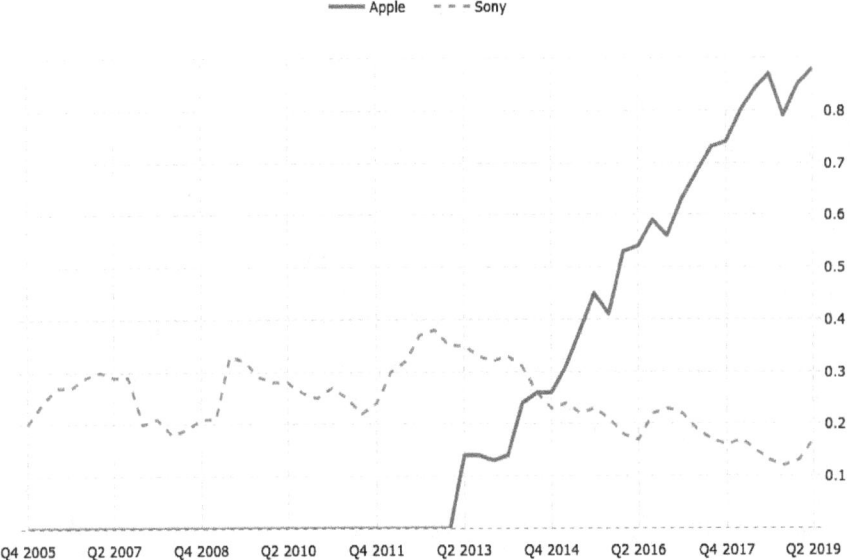

(Source: Macrotrends)

From a strategic perspective, this is one of the reasons portfolio managers must be more proactive and watch for insider trading signals as a way to consistently identify opportunities for superior investment returns. Fortunately, these strategies also help income investors avoid unexpected instances of risk in the corporate bond market. But while this information is readily available for anyone interested in doing the research, most investors fail to capitalize on favorable investment opportunities that often follow major changes in stock buying or selling activities of high-level corporate insiders.

Conclusion: D/E Ratios Help Investors Identify Risky Investments

The D/E ratio can be a valuable tool for investors looking to identify companies that are highly leveraged and potentially vulnerable to increased risk in the event of a market downturn. For the best results, income investors should view a company's D/E against the averages seen in similar companies within its industry peer group. These techniques can help income investors gain a better understanding of the equity-liability relationship that characterizes the company and its bond offerings.

Of course, not all companies with a high debt-to-equity ratio will be conducting poor business practices. Debt can often work as a catalyst for expansion in the operations of a business and help a company generate added income for shareholders. However, significant negatives become apparent when a company's D/E ratio reaches extreme levels, as losses on the company's balance sheet are compounded down and the firm may find itself in a position where it is no longer able to service its financial obligations. When a company's D/E ratio is too high, its borrowing costs can quickly become problematic and this can weaken the long-term potential of its corporate bond offerings.

Strategic Approach: Identify Mischaracterizations in Credit Ratings

When designing an income portfolio investment strategy, the D/E ratio can be used as a tool to help identify mischaracterizations in the corporate credit ratings made available by the major agencies.

(Ratings comparisons of General Electric bonds and Twitter bonds)

- **General Electric - Credit Rating:** BBB+ (only recently lowered from A in 2018)

- **Twitter - Credit Rating:** BB- (equal to speculative-grade or "junk" status)

Long-Term Outlook: Based on a relative analysis of the comprehensive credit quality metrics at both companies, GE bonds should be rated lower than Twitter bonds. However, when we look at the ratings grades that have been given to both companies by the major agencies, we can see that this is not the case.

Fortunately, these mischaracterizations in credit quality create contrarian opportunities for those structuring income investment portfolios. As we will see in the following historical case studies, signals highlighting favorable investment opportunities can be spotted early using the actions of high-level corporate insiders.

Despite General Electric's Investment-Grade Status, Credit Quality Remains Vulnerable

In recent quarters, General Electric has made aggressive moves to lower its pension and debt liabilities. These moves may have helped Fitch, Moody's, and Standard & Poor's to maintain investment-grade ratings for the company.

However, any prudent analysis from a balance sheet perspective suggests General Electric's credit outlook is likely to remain vulnerable going forward (with the possibility of being assigned to junk status). Ultimately, the long-term deterioration in General Electric's credit metrics fully justify renewed ratings cuts for the company but these trends are not accurately reflected in credit ratings from the three major agencies.

GE's Failed Plans Have Been Overlooked by Ratings Agencies

In June 2018, company executives announced plans to make drastic reductions in GE's leverage figures before the end of 2020. When making these projections, management was able to identify available sources of cash which totaled $60 billion. Management explained that this money could be used to strengthen the balance sheet of struggling units like GE Capital and cut net debt in core industrial operations by about $25 billion.

After those projections were made, General Electric initiated drastic measures to reduce its total debt figures. These actions included slashing its coveted stock dividend, speeding up the sale of its stake in Baker Hughes (NYSE: BHGE), restructuring deals to combine rail operations with Wabtec, and agreeing to sell 49.9% of is healthcare business (up from 20% previously) to outside investors. Despite this extended series of desperate moves, General Electric has failed to solidify its balance sheet and management no longer expects to meet its previously outlined leverage targets before the end of 2020.

Fitch Affirms GE's Credit Rating Despite Recent Allegations

In August 2019, Fitch maintained General Electric's BBB+ credit rating despite recent reports released by a notable whistleblower which alleged significant financial improprieties within the company. In its decision, Fitch explained that the "mix of developments" that unfolded over the past few months "has not substantially altered" its base outlook for General Electric.

Of course, this perspective overlooks concerns expressed by many market analysts highlighting weaknesses that could result from various liabilities (including GE's long-term care insurance business, the value of Baker Hughes, working capital, GE Power and the aircraft engine and leasing businesses). In the past, Fitch has ranked the company in second place on its list of 16 "riskiest" long-term care insurers, citing GE's large number of policies written when costs of long-term care were poorly understood. However, it would appear that Fitch doesn't believe these issues are deep enough to materially impact GE's credit profile.

In response to these concerns the ratings agency has explained:

"Fitch already considers these topics in its ratings for GE, and some are highlighted as risks supporting the current negative rating outlook."

Fitch's current BBB+ rating on General Electric is three positions above speculative grade (which is commonly referred to as "junk" status).

GE's Insider Transactions Signal a More Bearish Outlook

At the same time, limited insider buying activity in recent years suggests GE's management team does not expect to see a sustainable recovery in these businesses any time soon:

Table 1. Monthly summaries of insider stock purchases, sales, and option exercises for General Electric Co (GE).

Trading Period	Insider Buying		Insider Sales		Option Exercises	
year-month	Shares	Value	Shares	Value	Shares	Value
2019-05	10,000	$97,500	6,659,852	$64,195,420	0	$0
2019-04	0	$0	0	$0	122,036	$0
2019-03	0	$0	49,904	$495,546	52,019	$478,574
2019-02	0	$0	0	$0	283,902	$0
2019-01	0	$0	0	$0	101,550	$0
2018-11	295,000	$2,783,250	0	$0	2,357	$0
2018-09	0	$0	0	$0	70,100	$0
2018-07	191,000	$2,490,640	0	$0	95,000	$0
2018-04	0	$0	0	$0	4,000	$0
2018-02	0	$0	0	$0	5,000	$0
2018-01	2,689	$43,446	0	$0	0	$0
2017-12	0	$0	0	$0	137,400	$0

(Source: Insider Monitor)

As the company's profitability outlook has deteriorated, massive long-term declines in share prices have made it difficult for insiders to sell the stock at materially advantageous levels.

However, these trends changed in May 2019 after GE stock rallied by 76.4% in a seven-week period. Rather than seeing this bullish momentum as a reason to be optimistic about the outlook for the company, insiders instead unloaded more than 6,659,000 shares (valued at nearly $65 million) once the opportunity to sell at favorable levels became available:

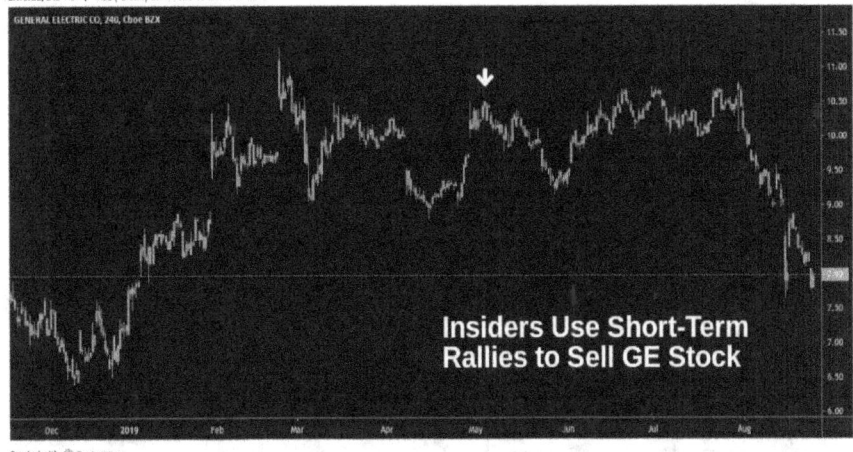

As we can see, this massive insider sales activity occurred during a single-month period and prudent investors should have viewed these decisions as a significant warning signal. When market conditions are characterized by frantic selling pressure, corporate insiders can alert markets to an increased likelihood that the company's credit quality profile may continue to deteriorate.

GE's Deteriorating Profitability Trends Remain Challenging

While consistently mischaracterizing General Electric's profitability outlook and credit quality, the major ratings agencies missed several fundamental weaknesses within the company.

- In 2018, General Electric's industrial operations finished the year with roughly $55 billion in net debt, which exceeded management's mid-year projections by $5 billion.

- These results materialized even after the company sold $3.6 billion in Baker Hughes stock (ahead of its prior schedule to do so).

- By the end of the year, General Electric reported results that fell below management's target for free cash flow by roughly $2 billion.

Clearly, there are several underlying reasons which help to explain why General Electric has been unable to improve on the negative issues that are visible in its balance sheet. Of course, the main problem has been a rapid erosion in General Electric's profitability over the last five years:

(Source: Simply Wall Street)

- General Electric is not currently profitable despite positive earnings trends in the broader market.

- General Electric's annualized rate of earnings growth has been negative over the last 5 years (at -65.3%).

- Earnings declines have accelerated over the last year (at -141.8%).

More recently, General Electric saw losses of $521 million in its renewable energy and power segments in 2018 (following combined profits of $2.5 billion a year earlier). These underlying trends are problematic because they indicate significant weakness in two of the three businesses that are expected to generate a majority of General Electric's revenue over the next several years.

General Electric's Inability to Meet Leverage Targets

As a result of each of these factors, it appears unlikely that General Electric will be able to meet its leverage targets by the end of 2020 —even if the company manages to reduce industrial net debt levels to $25 billion (in line with management's initial forecasts). Fortunately, income investors could have been alerted to these negative scenarios as they began to develop and made strategic portfolio decisions while declines in credit quality were still in their earliest stages.

Rather than relying on the inaccurate ratings grades given to General Electric by the major credit rating agencies, investors could have monitored negative developments visible on GE's balance sheet and used publicly available information detailing trading decisions made by corporate insiders as actionable investment signals. As we will see in the sections that follow, this tends to yield much better results for income investors in challenging market environments.

General Electric's Balance Sheet Assessments

Total leverage figures are measured using a comparison between debt levels and a company's earnings before interest, taxes, depreciation, and amortization (EBITDA). Sustained inability to show strength under these metrics tends to create negative scenarios for income investors assessing the credit quality of a company and the viability of its bond offerings. Despite the company's investment-grade credit rating from the major agencies, General Electric remains a clear example of this type of negative scenario.

In early 2019, GE's power, aviation and renewable energy segments (its core operations) continued to disappoint market expectations. First-quarter revenues came in at $15.2 billion, which marked an annualized decline of -5%. Within this group, the aviation unit was the only core segment that generated annualized revenue growth (with gains of 12%). Segment profit showed declines of -19%, while segment profit margin fell -200 basis points year-over-year (at 10%). All of this puts General Electric in a very vulnerable credit position if the broader economy experiences cyclical declines and segment performance peaks.

General Electric Credit Metrics
($ Millions)

Debt/EBITDA	GE Q1 '19	Q1 '19 Annualized	Biopharma	GE Proforma
Segment Profit	$ 2,658	$ 10,632		10,632
Corporate Eliminations	(204)	(816)		(816)
Depr./Amortization PP&E	1,249	4,996		4,996
Amortization of intangibles	463	1,852		1,852
Estimated EBITDA	4,166	16,664	(1,259)	15,405
Debt		107,526	(21,400)	86,126
Debt/EBITDA		6.5x	17.0x	5.6x

(1) At 17x EBITDA, it implies GE Biopharma EBITDA of $1.3B

(Source: Company Filings)

Potential weaknesses in General Electric's margins and cash flow create an uncertain environment for income investors, given the company's excessive debt load (at $108 billion). Even after the company sold its Biopharma unit to Danaher (NYSE: DHR), a strong argument could be made that General Electric's debt profile already dropped to junk levels. Danaher's purchase of GE Biopharma was significant due to the sheer size of the transaction (at 17x EBITDA, the sale totaled $21 billion).

Ultimately, this allowed GE to pare some of its debt while diverting the narrative in ways that kept the major ratings agencies focused on areas outside of its problematic financial results. If the major ratings agencies instead focused solely on GE's total debt/EBITDA, a very different picture would begin to emerge:

- General Electric's first-quarter 2019 segment profits (minus corporate eliminations, plus depreciation and amortization) came in at roughly $4.2 billion (proxy for EBITDA).
- Run rate EBITDA (annualized from the first-quarter period in 2019) totals $16.7 billion.
- This puts General Electric's debt/EBITDA at roughly 6.5x.
- As a result of the sale of the Biopharma unit, General Electric is expected to lose $1.3 billion in EBITDA and reduce its debt by $21.4 billion.
- This leaves General Electric with $15.4 billion in EBITDA and debt totaling $86.1 billion.
- This creates a debt/EBITDA of roughly 5.6x, which is a level that is **typically considered to be junk status.**

A debt/EBITDA metric that is 5.0x or above is typically considered to be weaker than investment-grade. Even with General Electric's sale of its Biopharma unit (which adds liquidity to the company's balance sheet) and all of the company's other extreme measures to shore up its credit profile, ratio levels under the debt/EBITDA metric still indicate junk status.

Thus, income investors buying GE bonds based on the biased analysis of any of the three major credit rating agencies could face significant risks in the event of a default on the company's loan obligations. Traditional balance sheet analysis shows General Electric's financial situation to be quite precarious. Problematic trends include the fact that the company has $259 billion in total liabilities, -$35 billion in net tangible assets, and has lost -$22 billion in net income over the last year.

As of 6/30/2019, General Electric had $92.81 billion in long-term debt, $56.12 billion in shareholder equity, and a debt/equity ratio of 1.65 (after reaching highs of 2.03 in September of 2018):

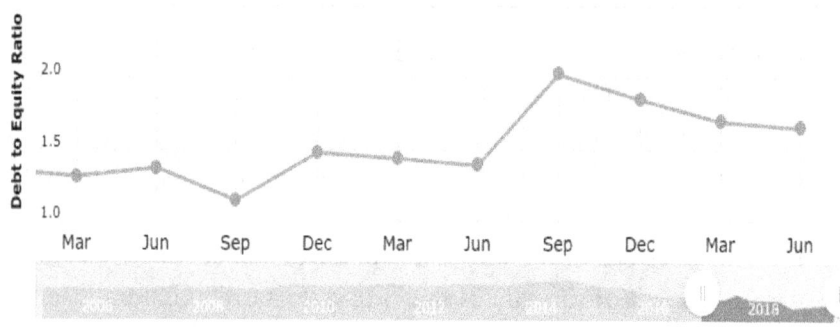

(Source: Macrotrends)

However, these negative trends in the company's credit quality profile might only continue to worsen. Going forward these are trends that should be viewed as problematic for income investors with exposure to the company's bond offerings.

Conclusion: Characterizations made by the major ratings agencies fail to reflect General Electric's true debt burden. These inaccuracies have the potential to put income investors at significant risk, given the clear vulnerabilities present in the company's credit profile.

General Electric's Continued Debt Burden

Currently, General Electric's debt level compared to its net worth remains elevated and this is a negative trend that has remained in place over the last five years. Despite its position as one of the most storied companies in the history of the U.S. financial market, these figures show that General Electric has experienced many difficulties with its proposed turnaround efforts.

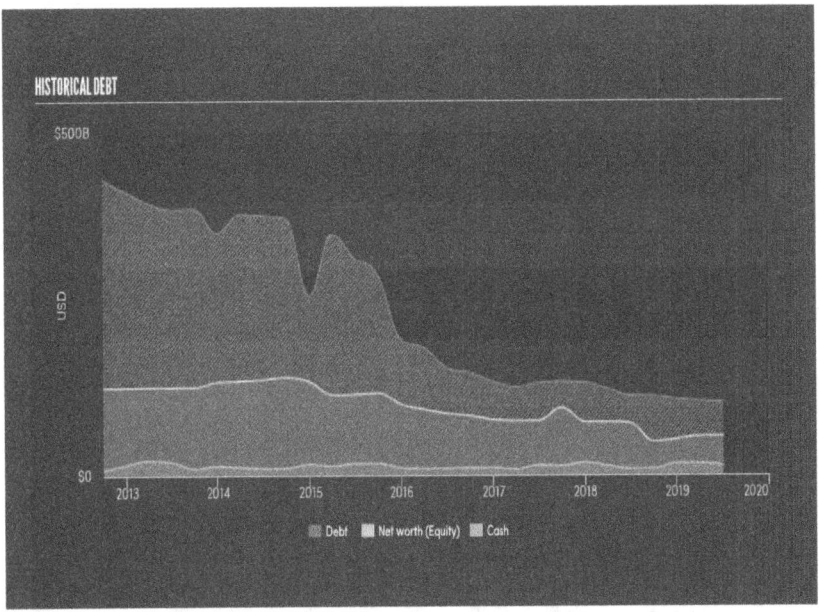

(Source: Simply Wall Street)

- General Electric's level of debt compared to net worth has been reduced over the past 5 years (270.3% versus 188.5% today).
- However, the company's level of debt compared to net worth is extremely high.
- General Electric's debt is not favorably covered by operating cash flow (less than 20% of total debt at 4.7%).
- General Electric is generating losses, so interest payments are not favorably covered by earnings.

Given the company's long-term deterioration in several important balance sheet metrics, top-level executives seem to have focused their attention on plans to calm fears in credit markets. This makes a good deal of sense, given the trajectory of the company's prior strategies but these efforts have largely failed to reverse the long-term outlook.

Continued struggles within General Electric's power unit have put substantial pressure on the company's cash flow. Despite mounting concerns surrounding General Electric's massive debt build-up, the major ratings agencies continue to maintain investment-grade credit scores of BBB+ for the company. Ultimately, this is an issue that must be questioned and scrutinized by corporate bond investors.

General Electric's Upcoming Bond Maturities

When a company has a large debt load, it's critically important to have constant access to funding because this helps to ensure the ability to manage refinancing needs that tend to be encountered frequently. Ultimately, frequent maturities should be analyzed by income investors when considering potential asset selections in any corporate bond portfolio.

With $110 billion in total debt, General Electric is no exception to this rule. In 2019, nearly $8 billion in bond payments were scheduled to become due and a combined total of $25 billion in bond payments are scheduled to become due in the years 2020 and 2021. Despite these alarming figures, upper-level managers have explained that General Electric has a liquidity position that is "fully sound" when all its credit lines are tallied.

GE Debt Stack

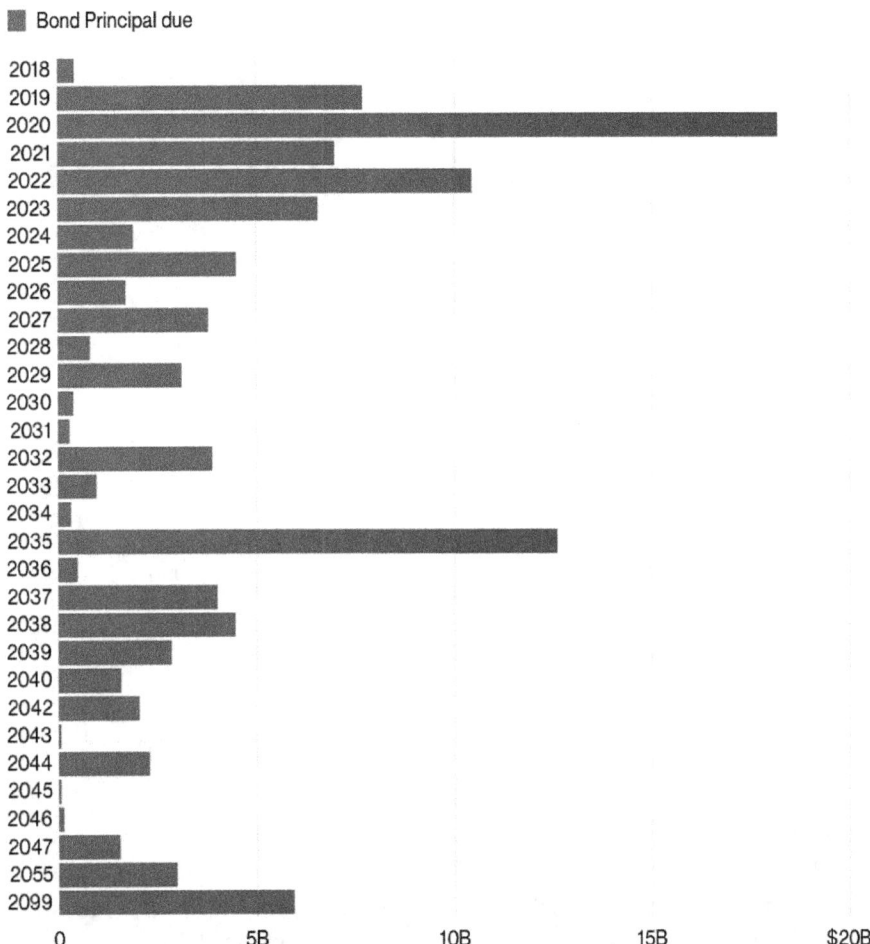

Maturities between 2048 and 2055 all in 2055 bucket. 2099 maturity represents perpetual debt

(Source: Bloomberg)

In most cases, these commentaries have been accompanied by further attempts at investor reassurance but there is still little reason to believe management is fully committed to fortifying the company's balance sheet through continued reductions in debt.

However, as we will see next, a visual representation of General Electric's credit profile seems to call many of these assertions into question.

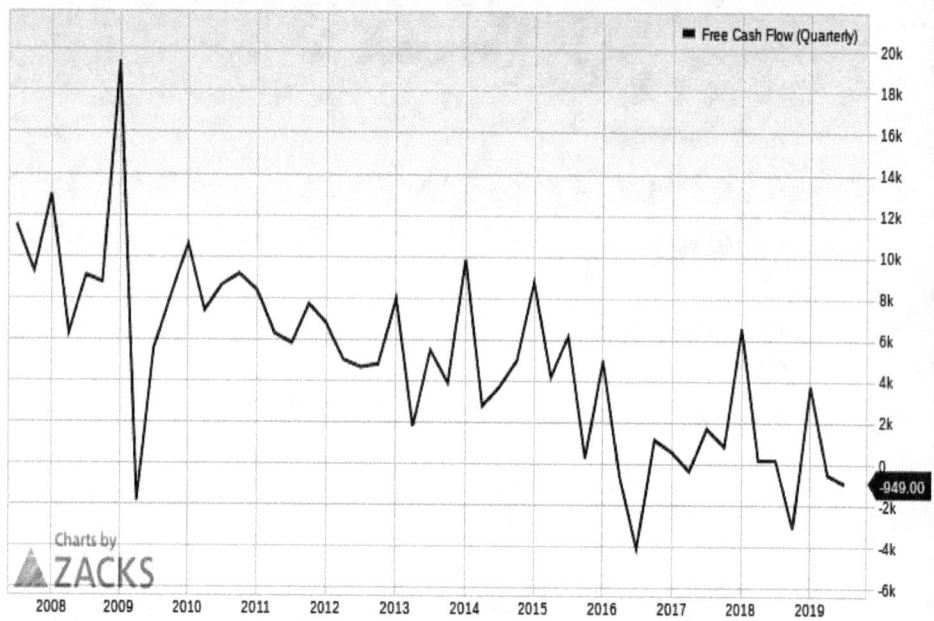

(Source: Zacks)

For corporate bond investors, important concerns lie in the fact that a substantial portion of General Electric's upcoming debt maturities (roughly $50 billion) become due over the next few years.

With quarterly earnings results showing continued evidence of weakness, the near-term proximity of General Electric's upcoming liabilities suggests that the company could be at risk of default even though the major ratings agencies have characterized its bond offerings as investment-grade.

Assessing Key Financial Factors

Over the long-term, General Electric's current debt distribution has painted an alarming picture for corporate bond investors. To put General Electric's substantial debt burden into perspective, the $50 billion in maturities that become due over the next five years represents nearly half of the total debt figure that will face the company in the future.

General Electric's highly leveraged financial structure (particularly its finance arm, GE Capital) has been questioned and criticized by many market analysts. At the same time, it could still be noted that some of the company's debt strategies have shown evidence of encouraging progress. In 2017, General Electric had $135 billion in total debt. Directed strategies to reduce borrowing and make a clear transition to sell assets has helped to drive improvements in the company's balance sheet. Since the end of 2010, the company has cut its combined short-term and long-term liability figures by roughly $300 billion.

However, recent comparisons to General Electric's free cash flow continue to mark an area of concern for investors. As of 6/30/2019, the company's free cash flow figure was -$949 million, which indicates a sharp decline from the $11 billion in free cash flow that was controlled by General Electric during the 2014 fiscal year. These concerns over General Electric's debt problems began to grow at a faster pace after Standard & Poor's downgraded the company's credit rating by two levels (from A to BBB+) in October of 2018.

Interestingly, Fitch and Moody's quickly followed suit and cut General Electric's credit rating less than one month later. Despite the fact that the company still held an investment-grade rating, General Electric bonds experienced sharp declines and several debt instruments hit all-time lows as these events occurred.

Has General Electric's Debt Burden Reached Crisis Levels?

Unfortunately, the company's new CEO (Lawrence Culp) did little to help prevent the sell-off, saying General Electric was experiencing a "sense of urgency." Rather than using declines as an opportunity to start buying stock, Culp only explained that management's strategy involved selling assets as a way of bringing down the company's crisis-level debt burden. Of course, these discouraging comments backfired and General Electric stock fell 10% in a single trading session (November 12, 2018):

Similar moves were seen in General Electric's bond offerings and the price of derivatives designed to protect against default losses in the case of a company default rose sharply. If CEO Culp's true intentions were to assuage mounting fears in the credit market, it could be argued that a more encouraging strategy might have been to start buying GE stock as it reached unexpected lows. When this did not occur, bearish activity prevailed throughout the market.

General Electric's Debt Situation: Just One of Many Problems

The long-term debt obligation that is visible on General Electric's balance sheet is just one of many problems that currently face the company. General Electric is dealing with a significant pension shortfall, its power business needs massive restructuring, and its reputation for stability at the managerial levels has been questioned after unexpected changes in the role of chief executive in 2018.

Many of the current struggles at General Electric (including the company's heavy debt burden) are long-term in nature and can be traced back to events that occurred over a decade ago. This was when the company's GE Capital unit accepted bailout funds from Warren Buffett and the U.S. government during the 2008 financial crisis.

In the periods that followed, General Electric's conglomerate model (which relies on strong businesses to balance negatives experienced in problem units) has continually misfired. General Electric's Power unit has consistently produced weaker-than-expected earnings results and these negatives have put increased strain on the company's best-performing units. Disjointed performances in many of General Electric's businesses have disrupted management's efforts to sell-off assets, reduce the size of the total company, and to simplify its structure.

In 2018, General Electric was delisted from the Dow Jones Industrial Average for the first time in 110 years. The company currently trades with a market cap of $79.2 billion, which indicates a decline of more than 80% from the $400 billion market cap that characterized when widely renowned CEO Jack Welch left General Electric in 2001. At this stage, it's clear the market has responded to the continuous series of unfortunate events that has plagued the company for nearly two decades —even while the major ratings agencies have maintained investment-grade credit scores for General Electric's bond offerings.

Deeper Concerns in Corporate Bond Markets

As interest rates continue to rise, credit markets have been nervous about the number of firms with substantial debt burdens evident on their balance sheets. Currently, credit markets show roughly $3 trillion in borrowings with a rating of BBB (the lowest investment-grade rating).

Following the 2008 financial crisis, these alarming trends have emerged as historically low interest rates encouraged companies to borrow more cash as a way of funding corporate buyouts of industry competitors. In corporate credit markets, the main concern is that many of these heavily indebted large-cap companies might already satisfy the criteria that are typically required before being classified with a "junk" status rating.

Were it not for the leniency that is currently being provided by the major credit raters, companies like General Electric would not be able to claim an investment-grade credit profile. Given the state of General Electric's balance sheet, it's not surprising that many analysts have been quite vocal in these criticisms with respect to the company's future growth prospects.

Scott Minerd ✓
@ScottMinerd

The selloff in GE is not an isolated event. More investment grade credits to follow. The slide and collapse in investment grade debt has begun.

9:25 AM · Nov 13, 2018 · Sprout Social

293 Retweets   551 Likes

(Source: Twitter)

Chairman of Guggenheim Partners, Scott Minerd, crystallized these sentiments in a Twitter message on November 13, 2018, in which he said the credit deterioration at General Electric "is not an isolated event" because "the slide and collapse in investment-grade debt has begun."

Should General Electric Expect Ratings Cuts?

Whether or not the major ratings agencies will follow suit and provide a more accurate credit assessment for General Electric still remains to be seen. For investors, the most critical piece of information lies in the fact that the market is already pricing General Electric's rising risk of default. Moreover, corporate insiders at the firm have taken action to sell the company's stock in a clear vote of no-confidence with respect to the future outlook.

All three credit rating agencies have released statements indicating no downgrades are imminent, even after recent reports alleging significant financial improprieties within the company. However, according to data from the Bloomberg Barclays index, yields on some General Electric bonds have already hit levels that are associated with junk-rated bonds. General Electric's only preferred stock yields more than some of the market's distressed credits, and prices of General Electric's debt and credit derivatives are holding near those of lower-rated financial securities.

In 2018, analysts from Moody's explained that General Electric's free cash flow would continue to be "very weak" due to the dismal earnings performance in the GE Power unit. The only strategy to balance these negative trends has been a reduction in shareholder dividends and Moody's warned of the potential for further credit downgrades if General Electric experienced weaker support from investors with respect to future corporate debt issuance.

General Electric's Long-Term Trends Reveal Further Weaknesses

Even with all of the restructuring strategies put in place by upper-level management, General Electric isn't making a profit and their annualized rate of earnings growth has been negative during the past five years:

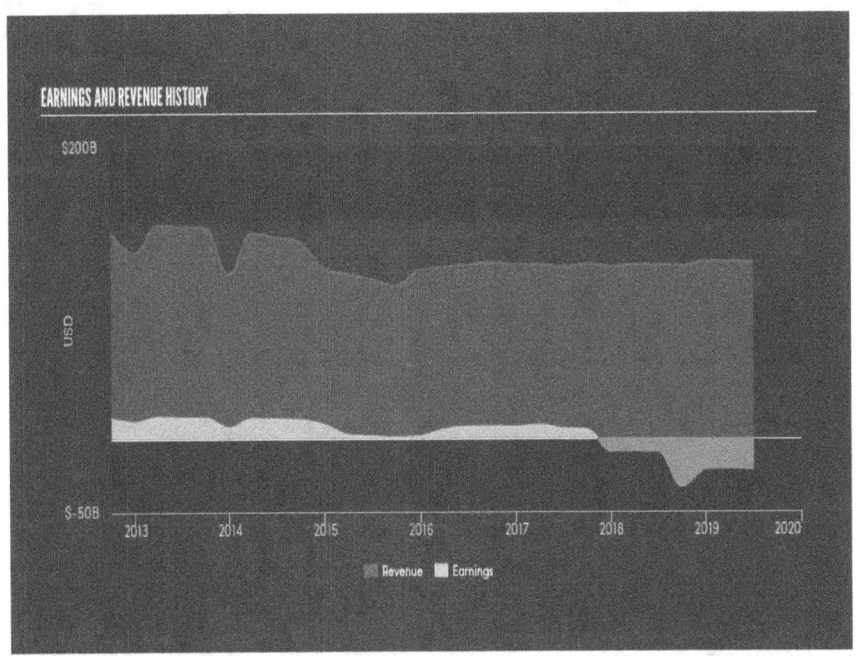

(Source: Simply Wall Street)

When General Electric's continued declines in net worth are combined with its persistent debt issues, it becomes very difficult for investors to justify the investment-grade credit rating the company holds with each of the major ratings agencies:

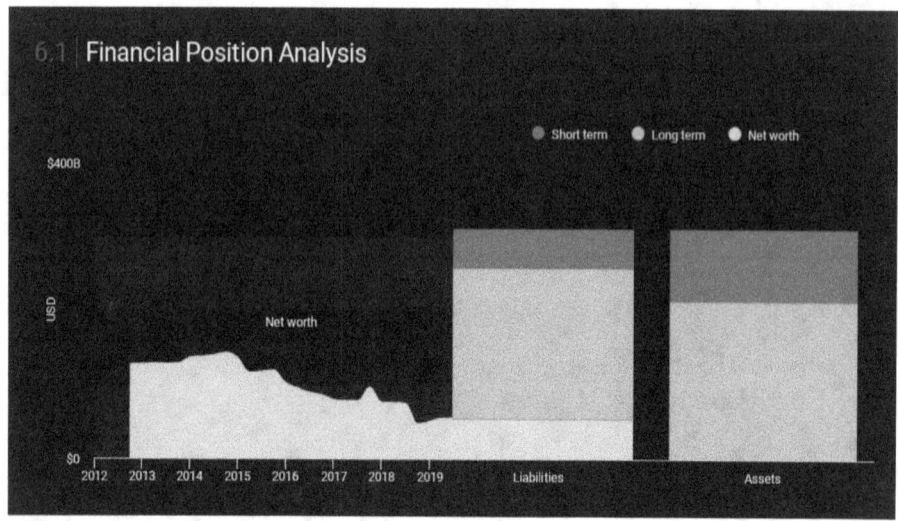

(Source: Simply Wall Street)

Overall, General Electric's long-term commitments exceed its level of available cash and other short-term assets. This is a persistent, long-term scenario that should send warning signals to income investors with current exposure to General Electric's corporate bond offerings. General Electric's extreme debt level is not covered by its short-term assets (the company's assets represent 0.9x debt).

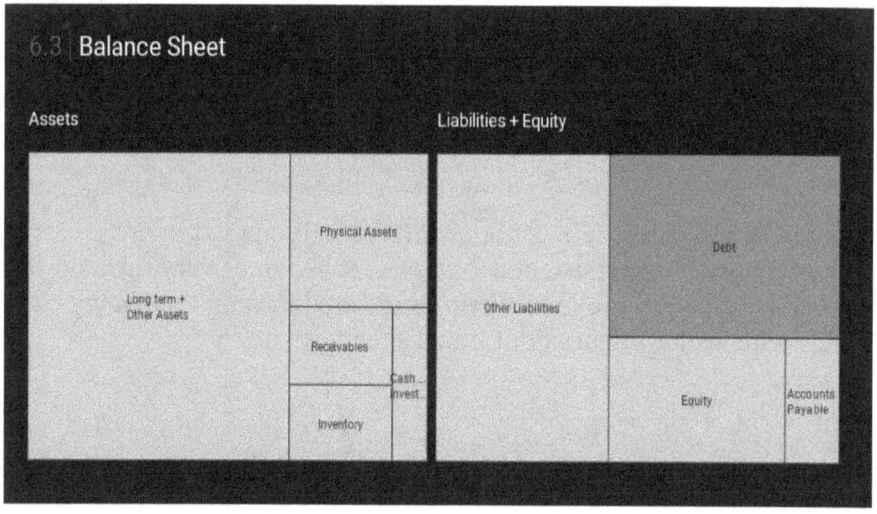

(Source: Simply Wall Street)

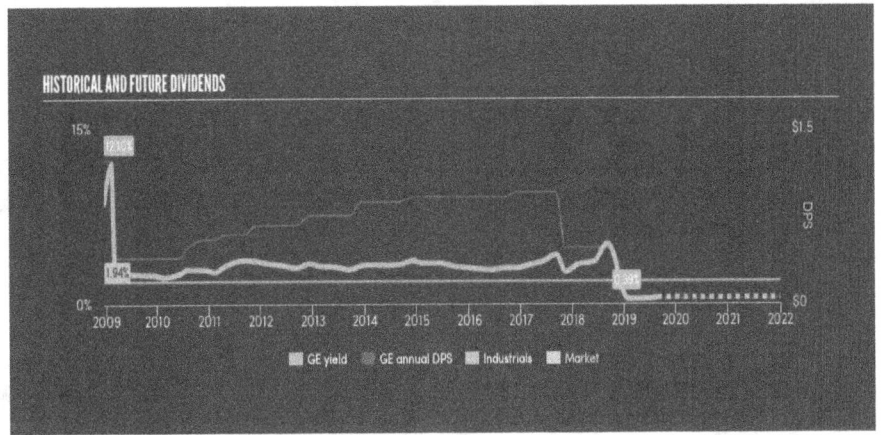

(Source: Simply Wall Street)

Ultimately, General Electric's desperate financial situation forced the company to cut its stock's coveted dividend to near-zero levels in October 2018 and forward earnings expectations show limited growth prospects into 2022.

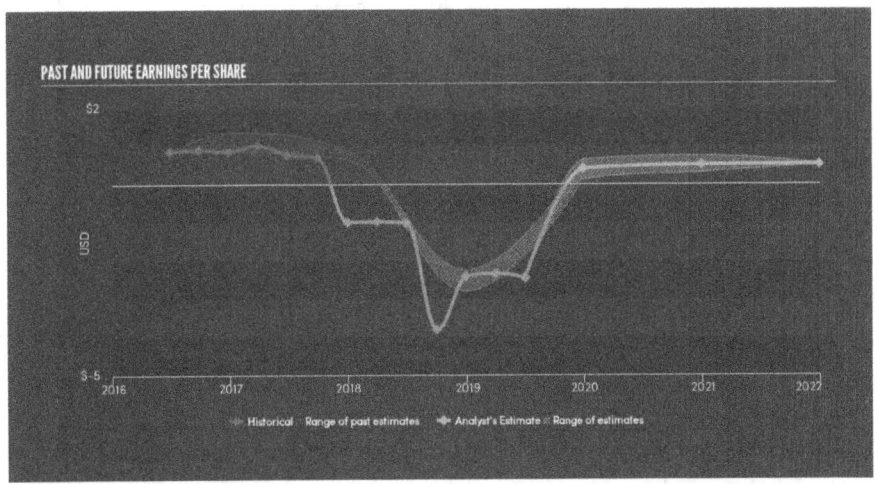

(Source: Simply Wall Street)

Even after General Electric's long-term trend in earnings growth is expected to move back into positive territory, guidance expectations remain flat for the foreseeable future.

Finally, a clear lack of stock buying activity amongst corporate insiders suggests that the credit profile of General Electric is unlikely to improve in the coming quarters:

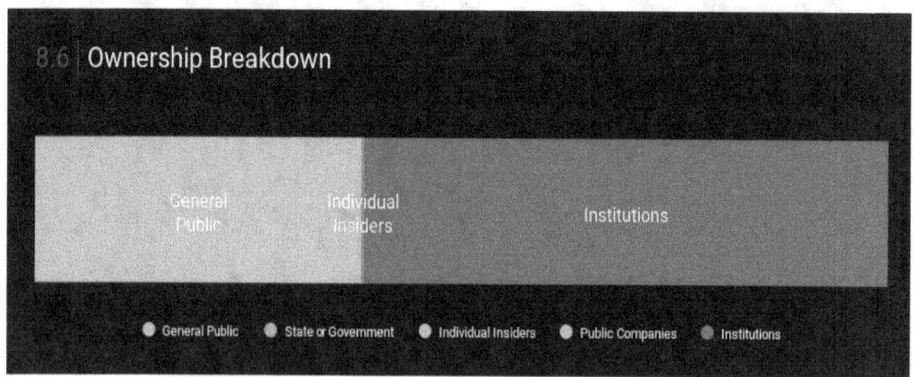

(Source: Simply Wall Street)

- **Financial Institutions** - Holdings: 61.32% (5,348,148,889 shares)
- **General Public** - Holdings: 38.53% (3,360,601,330 shares)
- **Individual Insiders** - Holdings: 0.14% (12,457,767 shares)

This overall lack of insider buying activity indicates extreme weaknesses in corporate credit quality despite the investment-grade ratings General Electric has received from the major ratings agencies. Currently, corporate insiders at General Electric hold less than 13 million shares of GE stock (which is equal to just 0.14% of the company's total value).

Conclusion

Despite its position as one of the most storied companies in the history of the U.S. financial market, mounting concerns surrounding General Electric's massive debt build-up have remained persistent. General Electric has experienced many obstacles and unexpected difficulties in its proposed turnaround efforts and struggles within General Electric's power unit have put substantial pressure on the company's cash flow numbers.

But even with all of this evidence of deterioration in several important balance sheet metrics, the major ratings agencies continue to maintain (and re-affirm) investment-grade credit scores for General Electric. This is why General Electric's management team must first calm fears in credit markets before income investors can feel comfortable buying the company's bonds. As a result, these are issues that will continue to be watched by corporate bond investors for many quarters to come.

Comparative Credit Quality Analysis: Twitter (NASDAQ:TWTR)

In contrast, Twitter has total liabilities of roughly $4 billion and the company is on pace to generate over $1 billion in operating cash flow over the next year. As a result of these positive trends, Twitter's bond offerings should be perceived as AAA. However, Twitter's credit rating is just BB- (below that of GE, which is a company in a much more perilous situation). These clear divergences between the two companies suggest strong probabilities that the major ratings agencies have mischaracterized Twitter's bond offerings (below levels that qualify as investment-grade).

For these reasons, bond investors should consider the following points based on Twitter's true financial outlook:

- S&P's BB- credit rating on Twitter materially overstates the company's credit risk.
- Credit risk is clearly overstated by convertible bond markets (with a convertible bond YTW of 4.2%).
- Twitter's perceived credit profile should be stronger, given the company's robust cash holdings and healthy recovery rate.

Twitter's Debt to Equity Ratio Has Shown Consistent Improvement

As of 9/30/2019, Twitter had $2.39 billion in long-term debt (marking an annualized decline of 8.39%) and $8.42 billion in shareholder equity (primarily cash and short-term investments). When we tally these combined figures, our calculations give us a Debt to Equity Ratio of just 0.28:

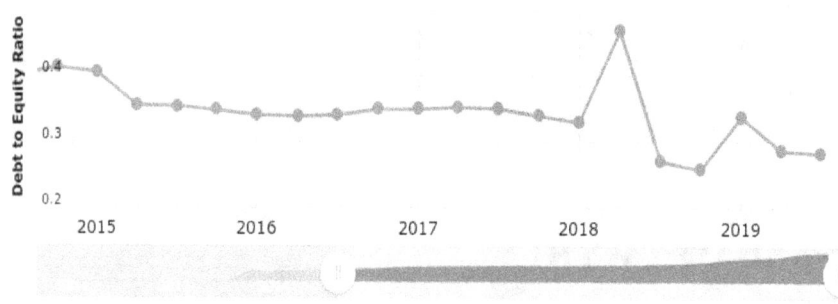

(Source: Macrotrends)

- Sustained trends show Twitter could comfortably pay off all debt obligations today (if the company felt so inclined).
- Twitter Bond Yields: 4.2% yield to maturity is quite compelling for a company with such a stable balance sheet.

CEO Jack Dorsey's Insider Buying Activity

Long-term growth trends at Twitter began to stabilize shortly after co-founder and CEO Jack Dorsey began conducting insider stock purchases at a fever pitch. In February 2017, Dorsey bought more than 400,000 shares of TWTR (valued at roughly $7 million).

In April 2017, he followed this activity with another insider purchase of nearly 575,000 shares of TWTR (valued at $9.5 million). The total purchase of 1 million shares (valued at roughly $16.5 million) in just over two months was announced publicly through Dorsey's personal Twitter account:

(Source: Twitter)

In the quarters that followed, Twitter experienced clear reversals in the underlying health of its key businesses. Many of the bullish operational trends that followed marked events that took the majority of the market's tech analyst community by surprise. For example, annualized changes in Twitter's advertising revenue flipped from negative to positive during the fourth quarter of 2017 and quickly shot higher over the next year:

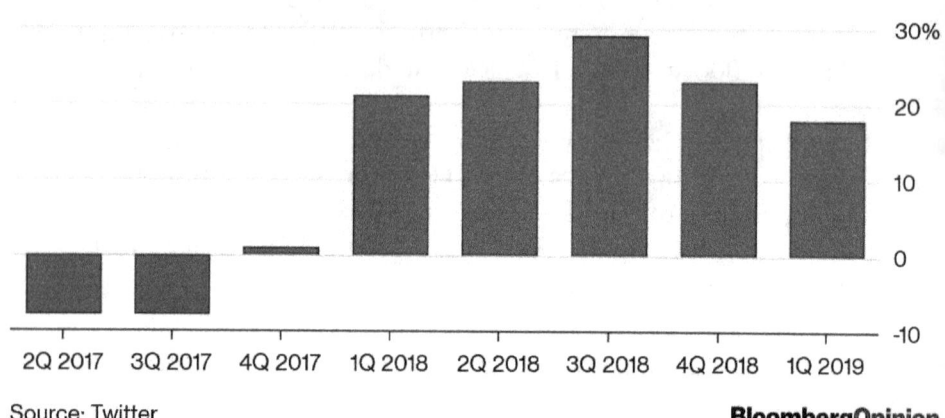

(Source: Bloomberg / Company Filings)

A closer examination of each of these quarterly periods can provide valuable insights into the ways insider buy/sell signals alert investors to contrarian opportunities in the corporate bond market. In these examples, we can see that income investment strategies based on relevant insider trading information made available by the SEC offer investors the potential to benefit well before major ratings agencies update the credit profiles of commonly traded companies.

Dorsey Initiates Contrarian Buy Positions in TWTR

To put these important financial reporting periods into context, it should be understood that shares of TWTR stock were still trading well below the company's IPO valuation of $26 per share when Jack Dorsey began his substantial insider buying activities:

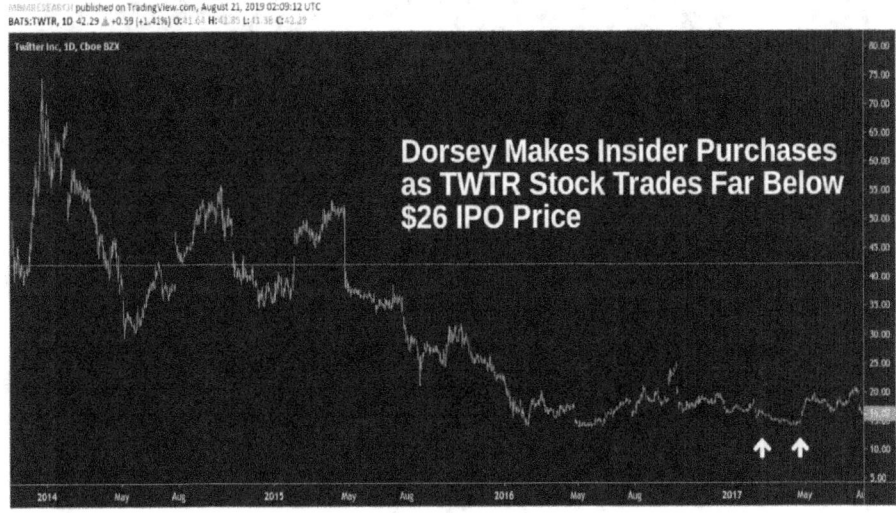

In 2017, Twitter's second-quarter earnings report led to declines in share price when it showed the company failed to deliver new user growth during the period. Specifically, Twitter's number of monthly average users (MAUs) was flat relative to the previous quarter, quarterly GAAP net losses posted at -$116 million, and the company's advertising revenue showed declines of -8% year-over-year. After the Q2 earnings report as released, Victor Anthony (internet analyst at Aegis Capital) gave an interview on CNBC during which he said:

"In Twitter, you have zero user growth versus Facebook reporting 70 million new users in the same quarter. It's not a recipe for a stock you want to buy."

After the report, shares of TWTR traded well below Twitter's IPO price of $26, so it's clear that this bearish view was largely present in the market's consensus. However, this was also the period in which CEO Jack Dorsey initiated massive insider share purchases valued at roughly $16.5 million.

Twitter's Next Quarterly Earnings Results

Q3 2017 - OCT 26 2017

After Twitter's next earnings report, shares of TWTR made an initial surge of 18%. Highlights for the period included positive surprises relative to analyst expectations for both earnings and revenue, while Daily Active Users (DAUs) rose by 14% on an annualized basis.

More importantly, management explained in its fourth-quarter guidance commentary that if the company reached the upper end of its EBITDA estimates ($220 million to $240 million) in its next earnings report, Twitter would be able to achieve profitability for the first time in its history.

Q4 2017 - FEB 08 2018

After Twitter's next earnings report, the stock quickly rallied by over 20% as the company's prior guidance projections were confirmed. During the fourth quarter of 2017, Twitter returned to revenue growth and **reported its first-ever net profit:**

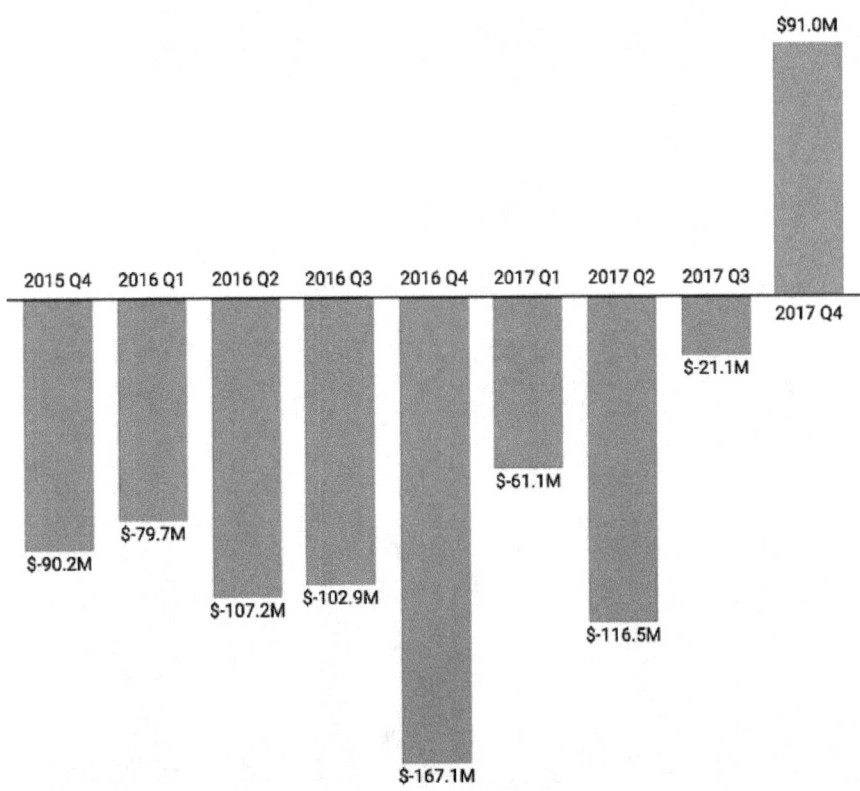

(Source: Company Filings)

For the period, GAAP net income was positive (at $91 million). Twitter's earnings of 19 cents per share beat analyst estimates by 5 cents. EBITDA for the quarter rose to $308 million (far above the market's consensus estimates of $241 million):

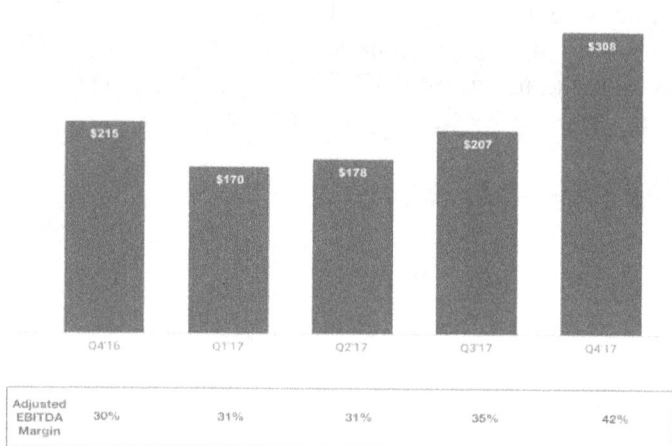

(Source: Twitter Earnings Presentation)

Revenue for the period came in at $732 million (beating analyst projections calling for revenues of $686.1 million):

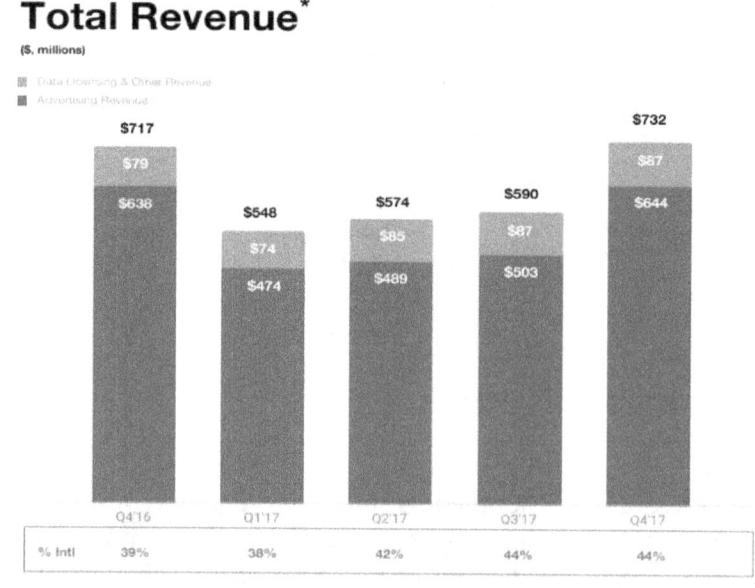

(Source: Twitter Earnings Presentation)

Following this pivotal quarterly earnings release, CEO Jack Dorsey released a statement saying:

"This quarter we made progress in three key areas of our business: we grew our audience and engagement, made progress on a return to revenue growth, and achieved record profitability."

For the first time in Twitter's 12-year history, the company was finally in the black. However, investors wouldn't have been cognizant of these emerging trend developments if they looked solely at Wall Street's consensus estimates or at the credit rating characterizations made by the major agencies.

Ultimately, no changes were made in the credit ratings by Fitch, Standard & Poor's or Moody's in the period that followed Twitter's long-term rise to profitability. But, as a result of these important earnings trend reversals, share prices in TWTR stock eventually surpassed the company's IPO valuation:

(Source: Atlas / FactSet)

Of course, these bullish stock market reactions trailed Dorsey's initial buy signals by more than six months. But it should be re-emphasized that even these belated market responses delivered a more accurate assessment of Twitter's strengthening balance sheet when they are compared to what was visible in the credit rating characterizations made by Standard & Poor's, Moody's, and Fitch.

This lack of action by the major ratings agencies might have been excusable if Twitter's move into profitability was a simple one-off event. However, these encouraging trends continued to strengthen for the company over the next several quarters.

Q1 2018 - APR 25 2018

For the first quarter of 2018, Twitter saw further gains in its share price after the company reported better-than-expected numbers for both earnings and revenue (EPS of 16 cents on revenues of $655 million). During the period, Twitter's revenue figure grew by 21% on an annualized basis. Following the report, Twitter CFO Ned Segal conducted an interview with CNBC in which he said:

"Sentiment [amongst advertisers] is much better, the ROI that they are seeing from their advertising on Twitter is much better based on lower cost per engagement and more ad engagement. That causes them to put more money onto the platform than they might have before."

Overall, this marked Twitter's second-straight quarter of profitability. Moreover, guidance commentaries highlighted management's bullish expectation that rising trends in advertising revenue would help Twitter maintain its profitability trends for the remainder of the year.

Q3 2018 - OCT 25 2018

Twitter stock saw its next significant move (immediate gains of over 17%) after the company reported adjusted earnings of 21 cents per share and $758 million in revenue for the third quarter of 2018. For the period, this marked an upside earnings surprise of 50% (relative to the consensus expectations for EPS) and an upside revenue surprise of 7.9%.

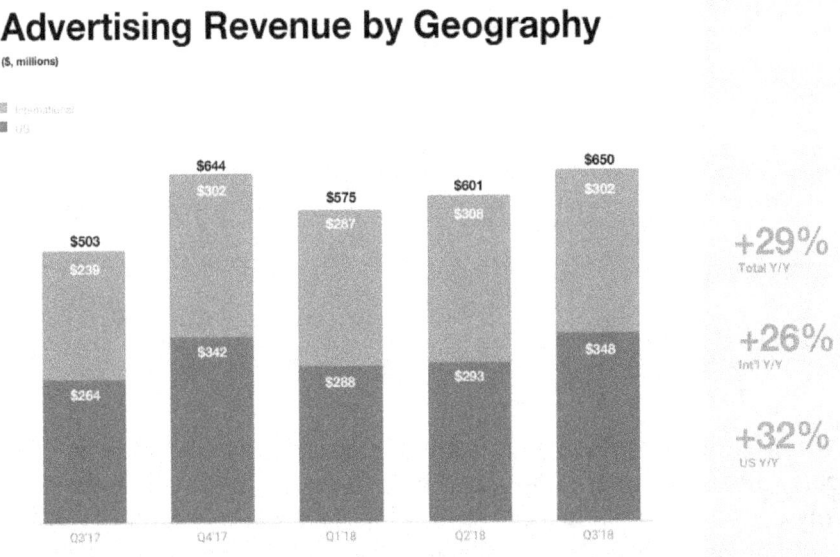

(Source: Twitter Earnings Presentation)

For the period, advertising revenue reached $650 million (which marked an annualized gain of 29% and a gain of 32% in component U.S. markets). Net income for the quarter rose once again (posting gains for the fourth consecutive reporting period):

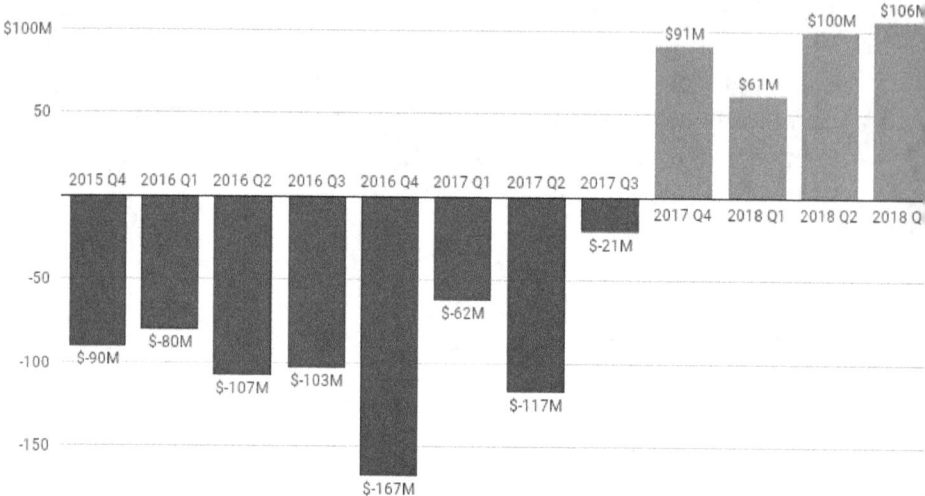

(Source: Recode)

Twitter's total revenue figure for the quarter was also higher by nearly 30% year-over-year, aided by a gain of 9% in the number of daily active users on the platform. This marked the eighth consecutive period of quarterly growth for this important social media metric.

Q4 2018 - FEB 7 2019

During the fourth quarter of 2018, Twitter reported the first annual profit in the company's history. Revenues for the period came in at $909 million, which marked a gain of 24% on an annualized basis:

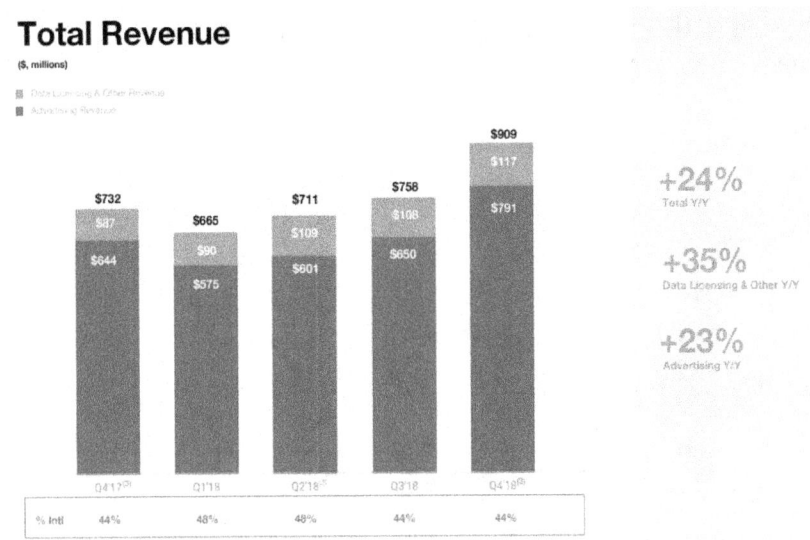

(Source: Twitter Earnings Presentation)

For the period, net income rose by 180% on an annualized basis (at $255 million) and GAAP operating income rose by 88% (to reach $207 million):

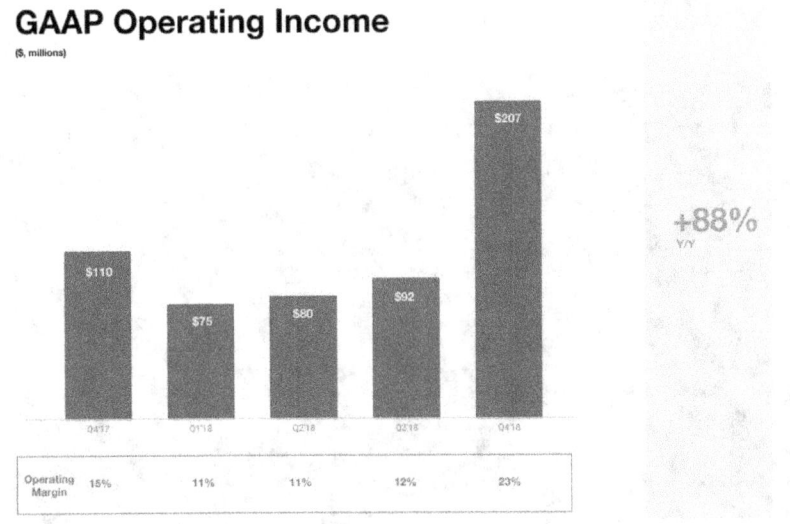

(Source: Twitter Earnings Presentation)

Adjusted EBITDA rose to $397 million, which marked an annualized gain of 29% for the period:

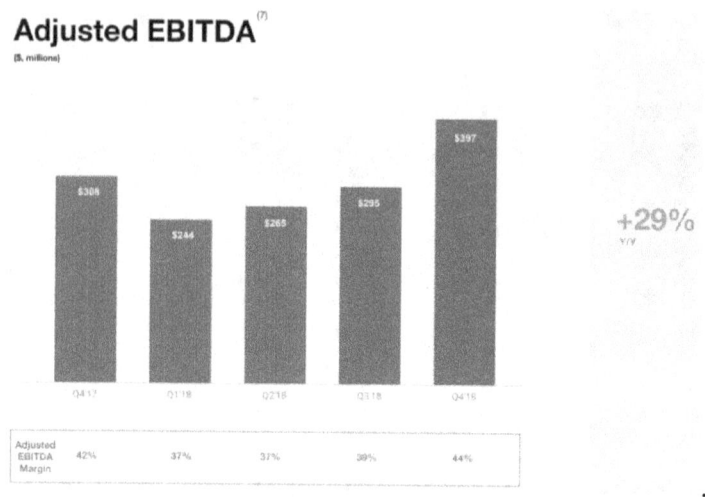

(Source: Twitter Earnings Presentation)

While Twitter's historic reversal in operations was making clear progress on several fronts, the broader market began taking notice of the growing strength in its balance sheet. As a result, Wall Street began ramping up its long-term expectations for the company and share prices rallied by as much as 98.6% in 2018:

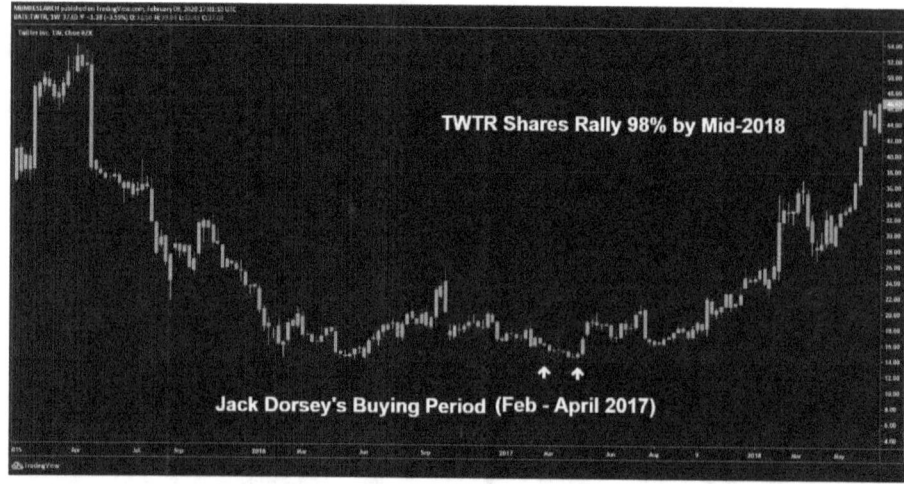

By the time TWTR reached its June highs near $48 per share, Jack Dorsey's insider stock purchases made during the first half of 2017 had **generated gains of more than 220%** in a period spanning less than 16 months.

One CEO, Two Different Insider Stock Decisions

Jack Dorsey increased his long exposure to TWTR just as he was selling an even larger number of shares in **Square, Inc.** (NASDAQ: SQ), which is the other San Francisco tech company he founded and continues to lead as chief executive. However, the most interesting aspects of Dorsey's contrarian insider trading decisions can be tied to the ways his actions signaled investors to emerging opportunities in Twitter's corporate bond offerings.

In contrast to the bullish financial situation that was beginning to develop at Twitter in 2017, Dorsey's top-level insider sales of SQ stock were initiated just as Square's credit profile began to deteriorate.

In the chart below, we can see that a strong spike becomes visible in Square's D/E ratio in the first half of 2017:

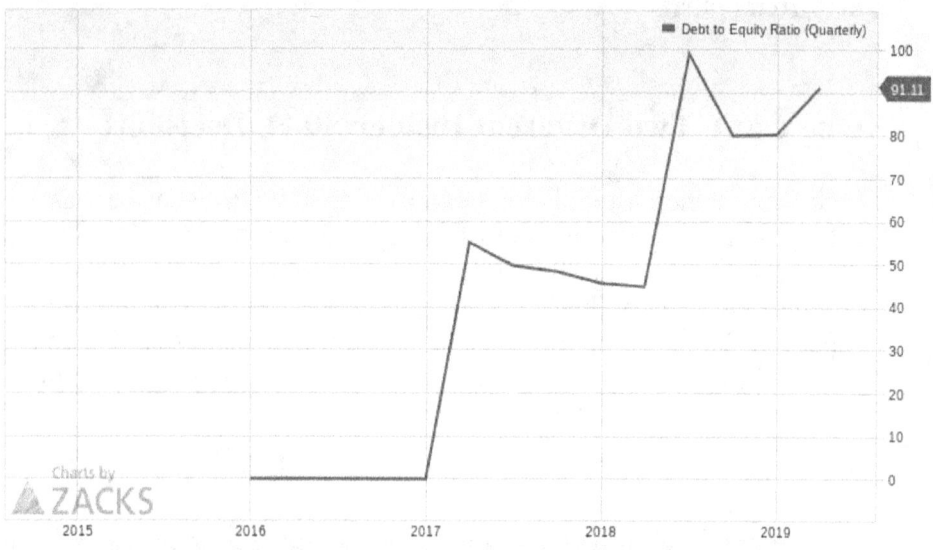

(Source: Zacks)

By the end of 2018, Square's long-term debt came in at a total of $0.9 billion, which marked an increase of 150.91% from the figures reported for 2017.

For income investors, this offers an important clue for assessing corporate credit quality. As CEO Jack Dorsey was selling shares of SQ stock, deterioration in the credit profile of the company quickly became apparent.

This deterioration can be visualized in the comparative Debt to Equity Ratios of SQ and TWTR:

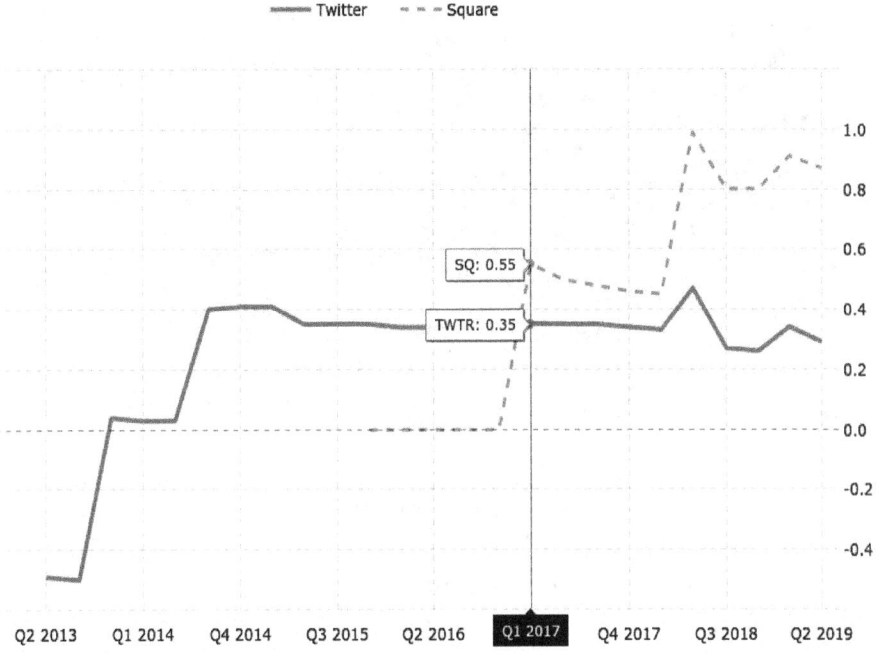

(Source: Macrotrends)

Ultimately, these diverging trends caused share price valuations to move largely as the tech CEO anticipated, with SQ share prices reversing lower from long-term highs while shares of TWTR were moving far above the IPO price.

Tallying Results: Jack Dorsey's Planned Stock Sales and Purchases

Jack Dorsey's TWTR stock purchases in February 2017 were conducted after a series of planned sales in shares of SQ stock worth roughly $11 million completed. Corporate executives often establish a schedule of planned stock sales as a way to avoid possible accusations of insider dealing (which shouldn't be confused with legal insider trades filed openly with the SEC).

In the period that followed the February 2017 TWTR share purchases, Dorsey sold shares of SQ five separate times (in two-week intervals):

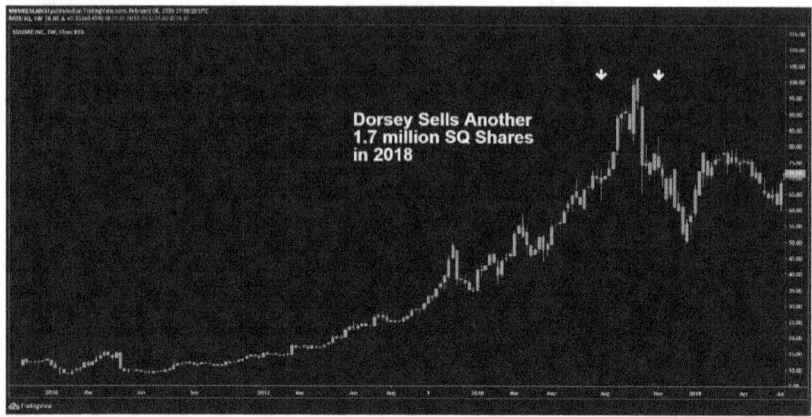

These individual sales of SQ stock (at 381,500 shares apiece) were worth a combined total of $31 million and Dorsey completed his second major purchase of TWTR shares in April 2017. In 2018, Dorsey sold another 1.7 million SQ shares of Square, netting close to $80 million after taxes.

During that same year, Square reduced its forward earnings guidance in six consecutive quarterly reports. Markets responded violently to Square's continued earnings disappointments and the stock lost nearly half of its value in the process:

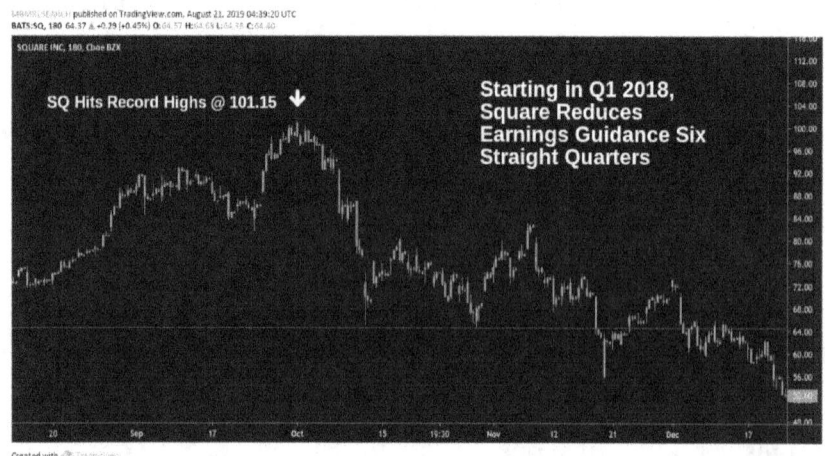

For 2019, Square is expected to grow its EPS figure to 77 cents (following a loss of -9 cents per share in 2018). In 2020, Square expects to show an EPS figure of $1.11. However, even these optimistic results still mean Square would be trading at 56x earnings at the end of 2020. Inevitably, this assumes a substantial rate of earnings growth (44% in 2020). Remember that Square isn't profitable (as of the end of the second half of 2019), so it's not entirely clear that these optimistic expectations are attainable.

Conclusion: Continued weakness in SQ stock (even as the broader market has rallied) shows that Jack Dorsey's insider selling positions have worked as leading indicators of both Square's underlying credit quality and the company's upcoming share price performances.

Long-Term Trends: Square's Credit Profile Decline

After Dorsey's position became apparent, Square's total debt compared to its net worth quickly grew to reach excessive levels. Over the last five years, the company's level of debt compared to net worth has risen from 3.9% to 81.1%.

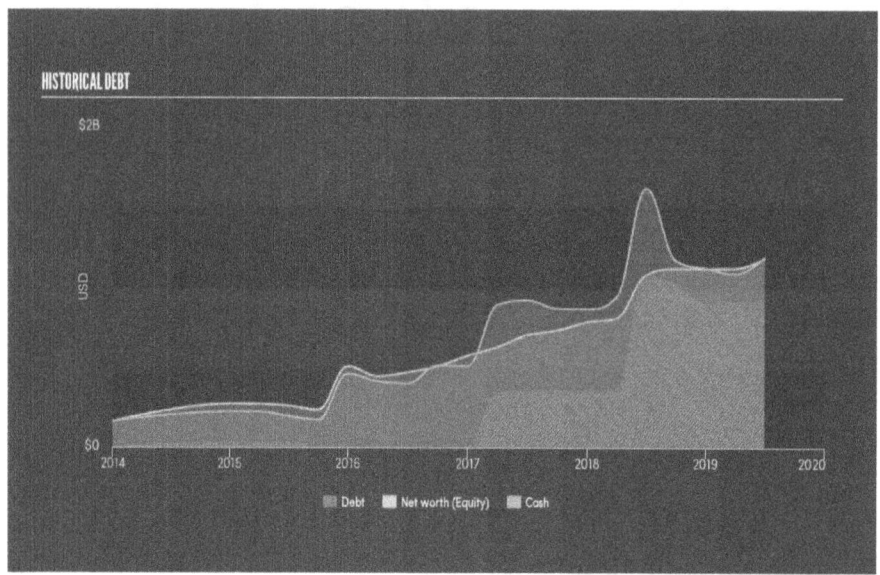

(Source: Simply Wall Street)

Nearly all of this debt at Square accumulated after Dorsey began selling shares of SQ stock during the first few months of 2017:

- Square's debt/equity ratio has significantly increased since Jack Dorsey began selling shares of the company.
- Square's total debt levels (at 77.6%) are high when compared to the company's net worth (i.e. much greater than the safety threshold of 40%).
- During the last five years, Squares debt ratios have increased from 6.9% to 77.6%.

Ultimately, this clear deterioration of Square's credit quality was preceded by bearish insider transactions that were far above anything present in the historical averages for SQ stock. Investors monitoring these decisions as potential buy/sell signals would have been alerted to upcoming trends in Square's credit outlook well before any of the major ratings agencies took the necessary actions to adjust assessments of the company's credit quality profile

Income Investor Takeaways

- Income investors should not view this combination of events as a simple coincidence.
- Comparative metrics in credit quality began to diverge as Jack Dorsey sold SQ and bought TWTR.
- Dorsey's actions signaled underlying credit weakness in SQ and new contrarian buying opportunities in TWTR.
- Waiting for changes in the credit profiles from the major ratings agencies would have resulted in missed opportunities for investors.

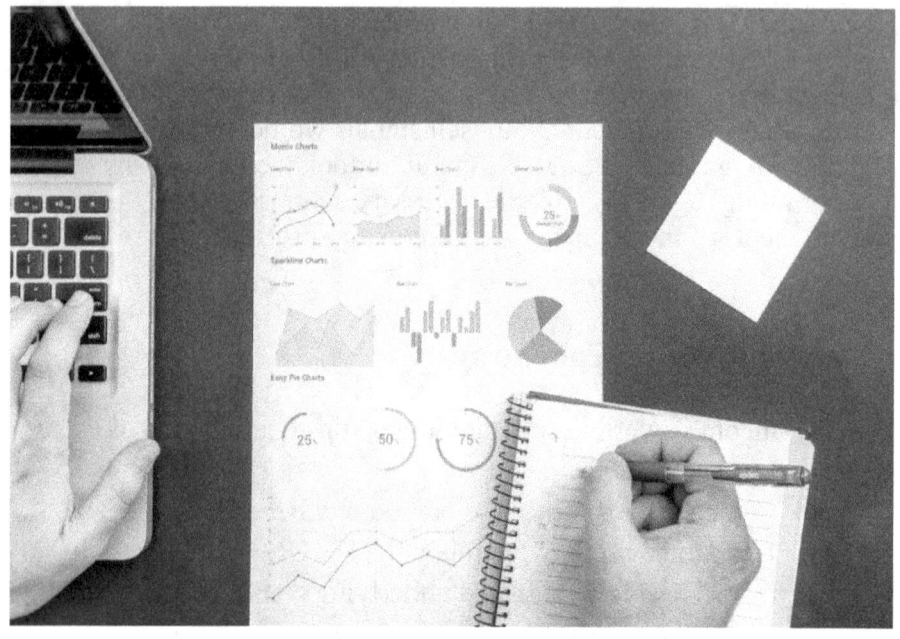

Forward Outlook: Twitter Could Easily Absorb More Debt

In most cases, corporate debt will become problematic when a company can't pay off its obligations (either with its own cash flow or by raising capital). As a worst-case scenario, a business has the option of going bankrupt in situations where the company simply cannot repay its creditors. A frequent (but costly) scenario can occur when a company is forced to issue shares at heavily discounted prices as a way to shore up its balance sheet.

However, one important negative that is associated with this financial strategy is the permanent dilution of shareholder equity. Of course, many companies effectively utilize debt strategies as a means to fund growth without encountering these types of negative consequences. Thus, investors must develop an approach to credit analysis that separates well-positioned companies from those with excessive long-term vulnerabilities.

Total Debt Obligations vs. Total Cash Available

When conducting an analysis to assess the debt levels that are most appropriate for a company, the first step in the process is to look at its total debt and total cash metrics in combination with one another.

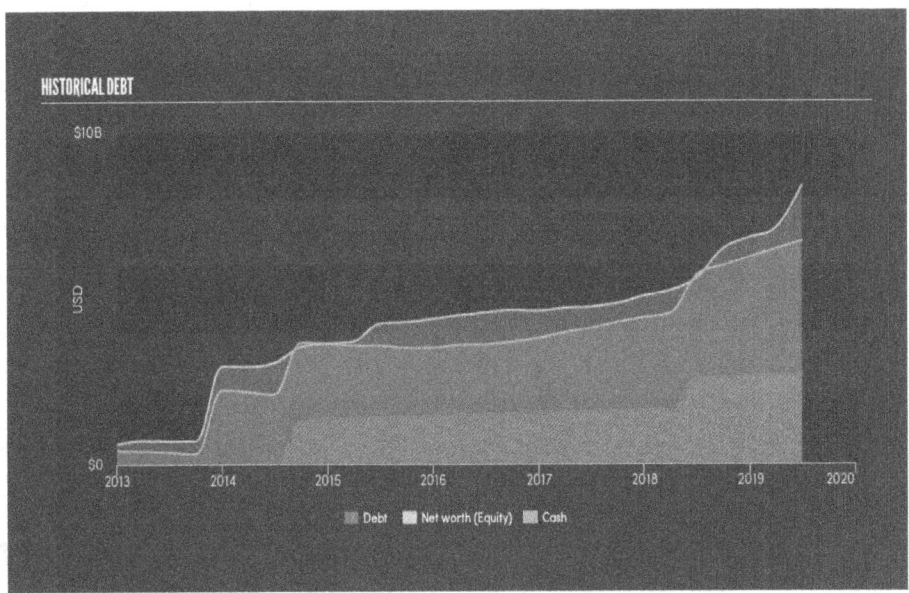

(Source: Simply Wall Street)

- Twitter's level of debt compared to net worth is below the safety threshold of 40% (at 32.3%).
- Twitter's debt level compared to its net worth increased over the past five years (32.3% in 2019 versus 6.6% in 2014).
- However, the company's debt is well covered by operating cash flow (at 54.4%, which is above the safety threshold of 20% of total debt).
- Interest payments on Twitter's debt obligations are also well covered by earnings (EBIT is 65.5x coverage).

As of March 31st, 2019, Twitter had $2.70 billion in total debt, which marked an increase of 50.8% from the $1.81 billion reported by the company during the previous year. However, these figures remain covered as Twitter's cash reserves have swelled to $6.46 billion.

Ultimately, this creates a net cash position of $3.73 billion for the company:

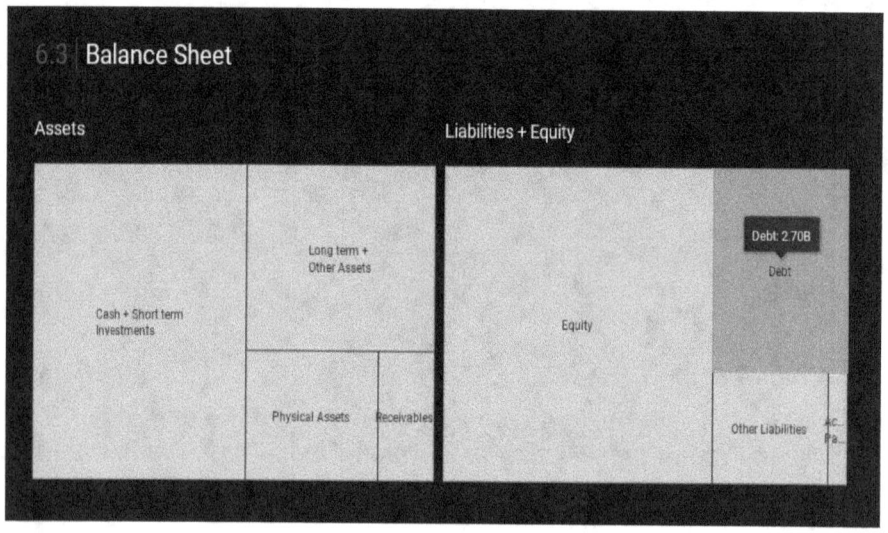

(Source: Simply Wall Street)

Twitter's debt ($2.7 billion) is covered by short-term assets (the company's assets equal 2.8x debt).

- As a company, Twitter is able to meet its short-term debt commitments with its holdings of cash and other short-term assets.
- Twitter's cash and other short-term assets cover its long-term debt commitments.

Assessing Twitter's Current Liabilities

When assessing candidates for inclusion in any income portfolio strategy it is critical to assess a company's ability to convert earnings before interest and tax to free cash flow. This can have a dramatic influence on its needs to issue new debt, as well as its capacity to manage existing debt.

Recent balance sheet analysis shows Twitter with liabilities of $1.62 billion becoming due over the next year. This upcoming repayment schedule is followed by liabilities of $2.43 billion which will become due after this initial one-year period.

At the same time, Twitter held $6.46 billion in cash and $684.2 million in receivables due within the next year. Thus, Twitter's balance sheet shows the company controlling liquid assets that are worth $3.09 billion more than its total liabilities. As a result, the company's short-term liquidity levels reflect a healthy balance sheet and show that Twitter can pay off its debts without difficulty. Even better, Twitter's earnings before interest and taxes (EBIT) rose by 177% during the prior year.

This is a highly impressive performance and it will give Twitter additional resources when the company needs to repay its debt obligations. Over the last two years, Twitter generated more free cash flow than EBIT. This is important because companies can't repay their debts using paper profits —they need cold hard cash. Fortunately, these figures show Twitter is a company with net cash on its balance sheet that is more than sufficient to meet its obligations.

Conclusion: Ratings Agencies Overstate Twitter's Credit Risk

As Jack Dorsey was completing sizable insider stock buys of TWTR shares, there wasn't much in the Standard & Poor's credit rating trend which indicated rising strength in Twitter's credit profile.

Prior to these events, the Standard & Poor's credit rating for Twitter was little changed from where it was following the company's IPO:

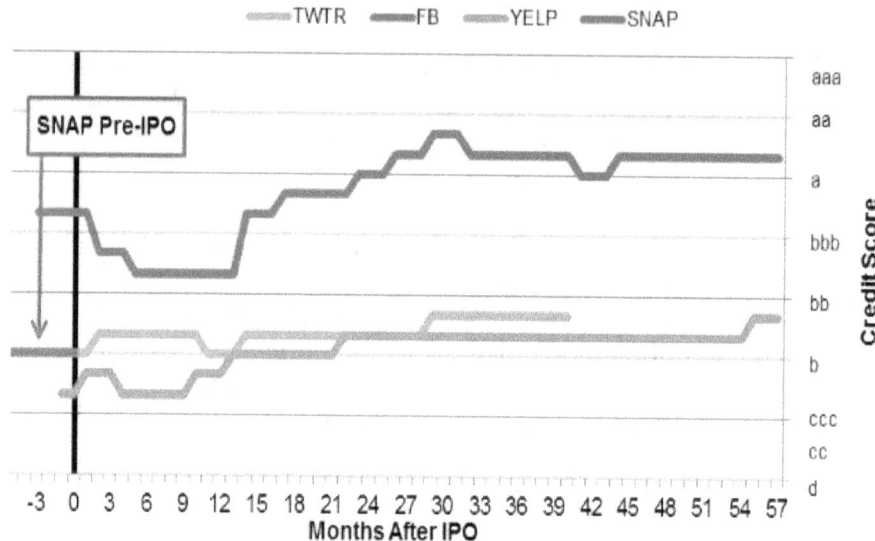

(Source: S&P Global Market Intelligence)

In any corporate bond assessment, it is important to analyze a company's total debt within the context of its ability to repay that debt. In the case of Twitter, we can see a company that has a fortress balance sheet and roughly $3.7 billion in net cash to protect its positive outlook going forward. Twitter's most recent performance figures show that the company converted 252% of its EBIT to free cash flow (to generate $975 million). As a result, it appears that the BB- credit rating from Standard & Poor's materially overstates Twitter's true credit risks.

Twitter: Consistent Insider Stock Buying Activities

Twitter's bullish performance trends are supported by consistency in the level of insider buying activity that has been directed toward the stock over the last two years. As part of a comprehensive portfolio strategy, income investors should consider these factors as being particularly important when assessing the comparative viability of corporate bond investments.

(Source: Simply Wall Street)

- **Financial Institutions** - Holdings: 72% (553,987,901 shares)
- **General Public** - Holdings: 24% (187,997,946 shares)
- **Individual Insiders** - Holdings: 4% (28,646,075 shares)

In contrast to the negative insider selling activities associated with General Electric (which faces continued uncertainty and clear weaknesses in its credit profile), top-level management has committed to much larger positions of ownership and purchased TWTR stock at a rapid pace. Corporate insiders at Twitter currently hold more than 28 million shares of TWTR stock (roughly 4% of the company). At General Electric, corporate insiders hold less than 13 million shares of GE stock (or just 0.14% of the company).

Twitter's 2019 Performance Trends Look Poised to Continue

Recent earnings reports have confirmed the validity of Dorsey's long-term expectations. Twitter's growth trends continue today, with several key metrics indicating sustained gains on an annualized basis:

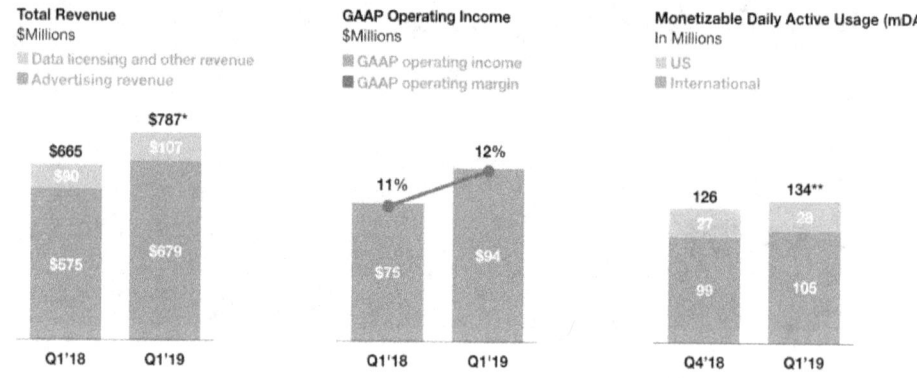

(Source: Twitter Earnings Presentation)

Twitter's total revenue figures grew by 18.35% on an annualized basis during the first quarter of 2019, to reach $787 million (which includes advertising revenue, data licensing, and other revenue). For the period, other important financial metrics also indicate strength for the social media technology company:

- GAAP operating margin increased to 12%
- GAAP operating income increased by 25.33%
- U.S. Monetizable Daily Active Usage (mDAU) increased by 6.06%

- International Monetizable Daily Active Usage (mDAU) increased by 6.35%

Long-term trends are relatively clear and investment exposure to Twitter may even be a way of avoiding the growing problem of stock market volatility. This is something that arguably would not have been said just a few years ago. Understandably, this might be difficult for some investors to believe, given the weak grades given to Twitter by the major agency credit ratings.

While it seems to be a company that many investors simply aren't noticing, Twitter might be the bond market's breath of fresh air. Long-term TWTR shareholders can testify to this effect and the company's underlying credit metrics continue to point in the right direction. Fortunately, Twitter also has managed to avoid the regulatory pressures encountered by many of the tech sector's bigger players (i.e. Facebook and Google). This puts the company in a favorable position even in an industry characterized by high levels of competition.

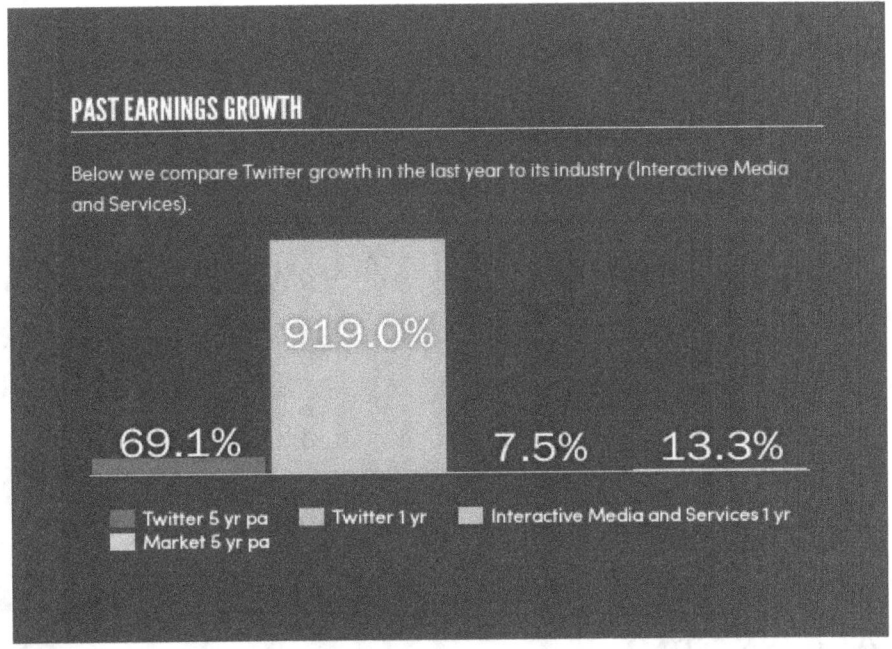

(Source: Simply Wall Street)

- Twitter has delivered annualized earnings growth of 69.1% over the last five years.
- Twitter's earnings growth over the last year exceeds its five-year average (919.0% versus 69.1%)
- In the last year, Twitter's earnings growth has far surpassed average performances seen in the Interactive Media and Services industry (919.0% vs 7.5%).

Twitter has had an excellent streak of positive surprises in revenue growth, and this has consistently translated into earnings growth that's just as impressive. In both areas, analysts' expectations imply sustained growth is likely to continue for the foreseeable future. Twitter's double-digit growth should be sustainable due to the fact that it's business model has not experienced the same types of regulatory attacks that have been faced by Facebook. Indirect rivals like Google, Inc. face regulatory headwinds of their own, as the company has been pressured to allow users to delete personal information Google monitored in the past.

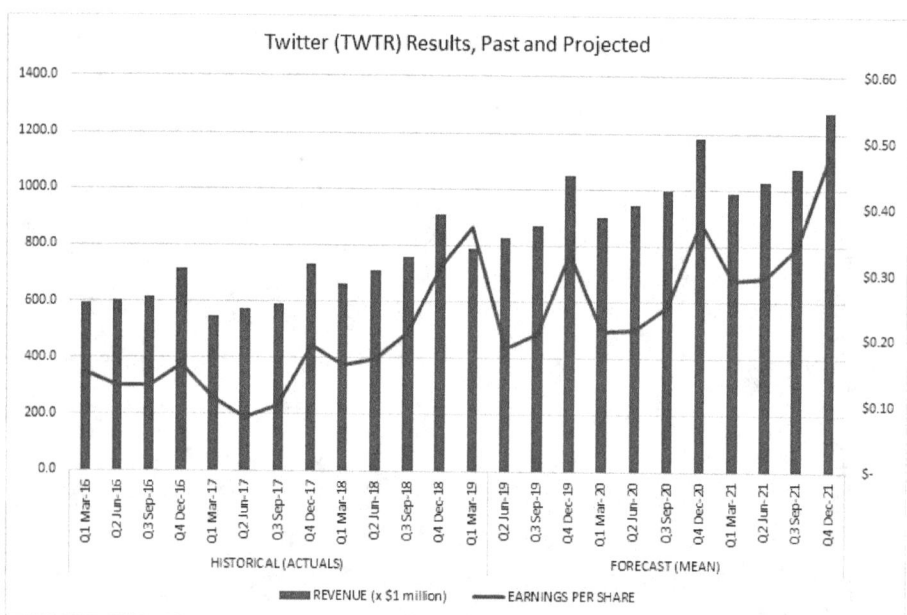

(Source: NASDAQ)

Advertisements seen by those users should, in theory, be less effective (and less profitable). However, Twitter hasn't been forced to take similar actions. Thus, Twitter's top-line and bottom-line figures appear to be much more secure than those of its competitors. Overall, Twitter's raw financial results should remind investors that the company is a standout in its industry and share price valuations should continue to pass the market's predictability/stability tests with flying colors.

Income Strategies: Insider Trading and Broader Market Direction

Many of the relative differences in the credit profiles of Twitter and General Electric could have been projected based on long-term insider buying/selling trends. Essentially, these examples show some of the ways insider trading activities can work as a superior indicator of credit quality.

Additionally, it makes sense for investors to analyze the broader historical trends when projecting future asset valuations. In the chart below, we can see an example of the ways insider buying and selling activities work within the broader market. Here, we can see that insiders typically sell stock (red line) much more frequently than they buy stock (blue line):

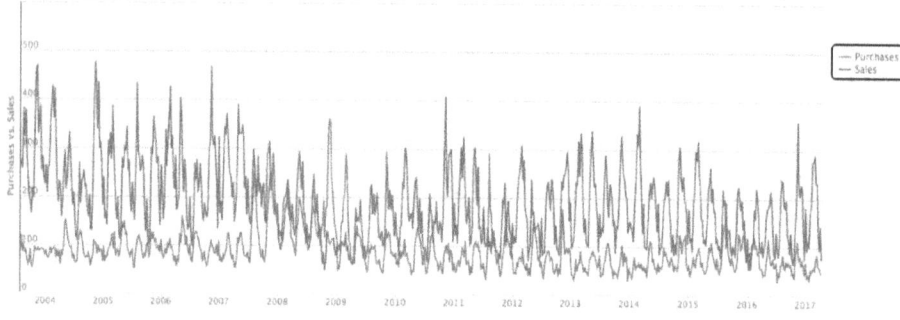

(Source: Option Insider)

However, when the trend is reversed it's generally an excellent buy signal:

- In October 2008, the S&P 500 traded near 800 (which was 15% from absolute lows following the financial crisis and roughly 50% from the prior-year top at 1,560).

- Spikes later occur in November 2008, March 2009, August 2011, August 2015.

Thus, the insider buying signal has been incredibly accurate at the macro level. However, signals were even more accurate during the second wave of share buying (March 2009 marked the absolute bottom in the S&P 500). Had an investor bought using this signal, the returns would have been quite handsome as the benchmark index tripled over the next eight years.

Insiders Often Signal Contrarian Investment Opportunities

After significant insider buying activity is reported, investors can watch for changes in the market's underlying trend as a way of measuring how equities behave upon the occurrence of such an event. The following chart shows this technique applied to the market. Essentially, these results show that insiders are often contrarian investors and their actions portend long-term changes in corporate asset valuations.

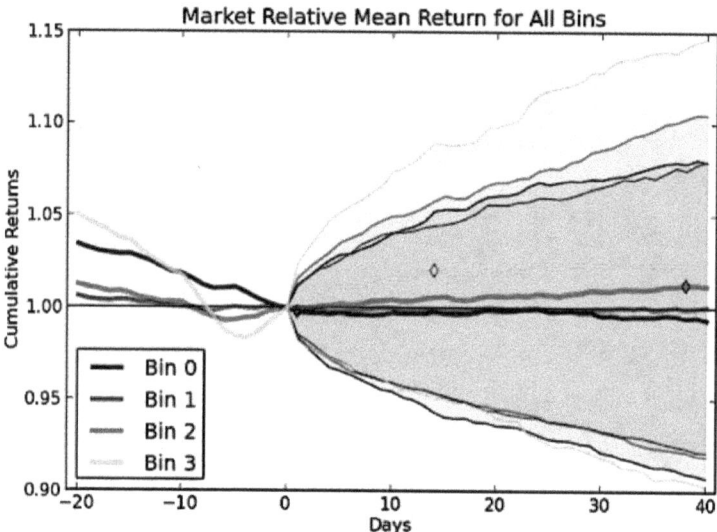

(Source: Lucena Research)

Results for various insider trading events:

- Bin 3 and Bin 2 represent **buying** events
- Bin 1 and 0 represent **selling** events.

As we can see in the chart above, results in the broader market averages contain actionable information that can be used by portfolio strategists when establishing positions in the market.

Conclusion: *Clear reversals are present in the dominant market trend after both buying and selling events from corporate insiders.*

This notable research study shows that positive event ratings tend to show greater profitability strength when compared to companies with negative ratings. Negative event ratings tend to show weaker profitability performances when compared to companies with positive ratings. In the chart above, threshold parameters show that Lucena's system ratings equal to (or greater than) 0.5 result in positive average returns.

Historical Case Study: Insider Buying Trends at J.P. Morgan Chase

Historical examples show that insider buying signals generate high rates of success when returns are compared to more traditional forms of portfolio analysis. In January 2016, J.P. Morgan CEO Jamie Dimon bought 500,000 shares of JPM stock (top-level insider purchases worth $26.6 million). The purchase raised Dimon's total holdings to 6.7 million shares (worth a total of $358 million):

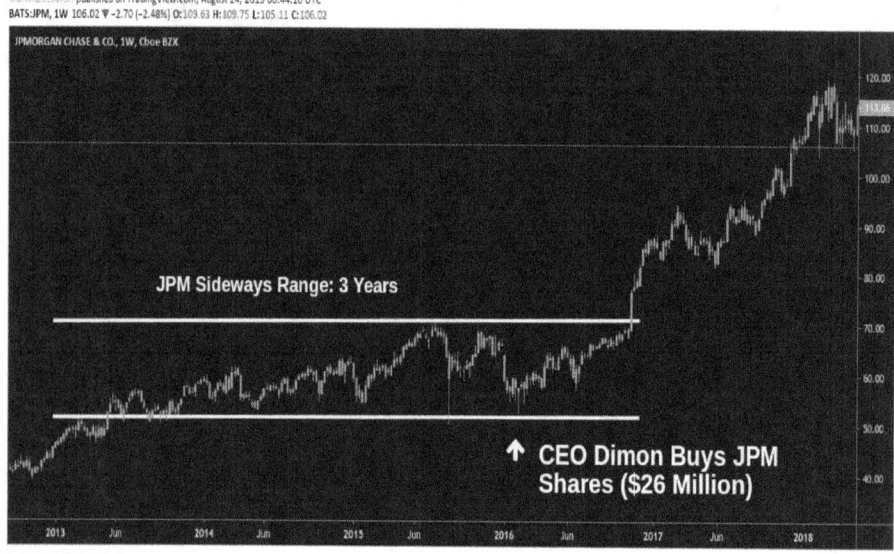

In this case, Dimon's purchase is unusual for a number of different reasons. In the chart above, we can see that Dimon's activity is essentially a contrarian trade that followed a multi-year decline in share price returns:

- When Dimon made his insider purchases, most financial stocks were taking steep dives while global equity markets were seeing heavy losses.
- JPM shares had fallen nearly 20% on a YTD basis and were trading 25% below its 52-week highs (these types of declines

were also persistent throughout the banking industry for this period).
- Industry rivals Bank of America and Citigroup had lost more than -30% for the year and had losses of -22% when the buying transactions started.

Fortunately, J. P. Morgan Chase was still a bank with healthy underlying fundamentals and $24.4 billion reported record net income in 2015 (a gain of 12% on an annualized basis). These trends helped the bank beat analyst earnings expectations for several years following CEO Jamie Dimon's insider buying activity.

- By February 2017, shares of JPM stock gained $34 (or 38%). This move alone raised the value of Jamie Dimon's holdings to $588.5 million (a gain of over $229 million).
- By the third quarter of 2019, JPM stock had gained by nearly 130%. The previous long-term chart shows JPM was caught in a sideways range from 2013-2016 but the stock starts climbing almost immediately after Dimon begins buying at an average price of $53 per share.

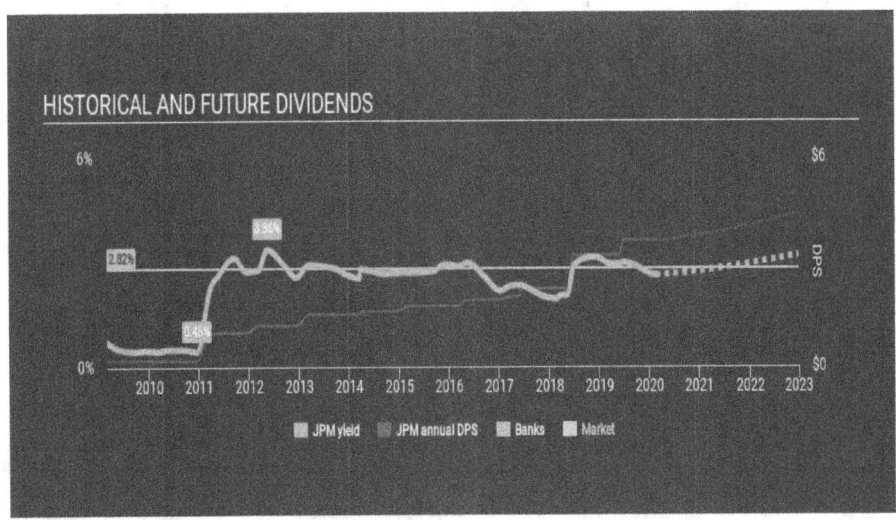

(Source: Simply Wall Street)

- While the stock's dividend yield dropped in the period following Jamie Dimon's insider buying activity, JPM still pays a higher dividend yield when compared to the bottom 25% of U.S. dividend payers.
- Dividends per share have increased over the past 10 years. This indicates strong underlying health in the company's balance sheet and these favorable trends rose sharply after Dimon initiated his insider stock purchases.

Outcome: *CEO Dimon captures excellent returns, as the stock gained nearly 130% by the third quarter of 2019.*

In this historical market example, we can see how insider buying can work as an accurate indicator of credit quality and potential gains in future share price performance.

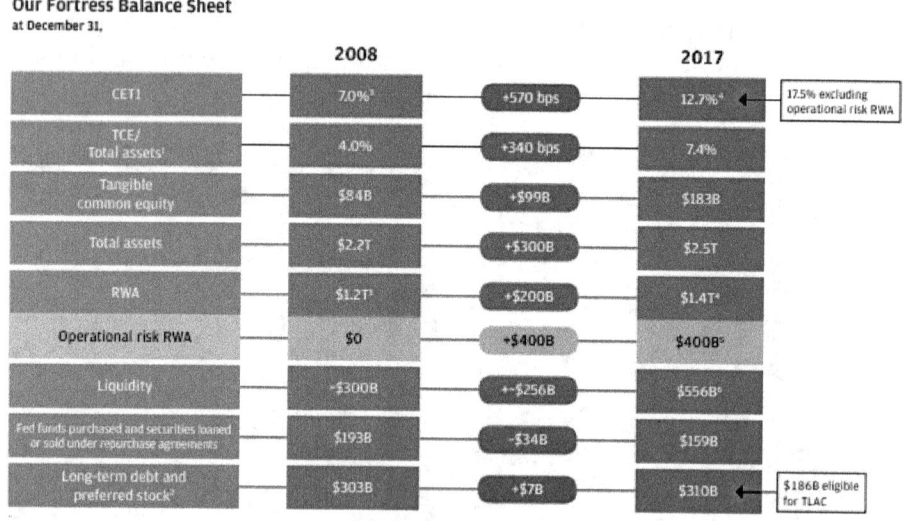

(Source: J.P. Morgan Earnings Presentation)

These results worked in favor of portfolio strategies while generating contrarian investment ideas capable of beating the broader performances in the S&P 500. In the charts that follow, we will see that J.P. Morgan's debt/equity metrics have improved steadily in the quarters that followed Dimon's substantial insider stock purchase.

Specifically, J.P. Morgan Chase closed a bullish performance the following year with a record-breaking quarter:

- Revenue from the bank's Investment-banking activities rose to $1.49 billion for the closing quarterly period of 2017.
- Total trading revenue rose to $4.52 billion (against expectations of $4.34 billion), indicating an annualized gain of 24%.
- Fixed-income revenue from trading came in at $3.37 billion (against expectations of $3.09 billion), indicating an annualized gain of 31%.
- J.P. Morgan Chase said that its strong performances were driven by improved results across all of its products.

Many of these positive trends can be visualized in the earnings per share (EPS) growth that became apparent at J.P. Morgan Chase following Dimon's buying period in 2016. Amongst the analyst community, these types of performances were considered to be relatively unachievable at the time. Rather than looking to the analyst community for accurate forecasts in these areas, income investors should have focused on the massive increases in insider buying activity as a central leading indicator.

In the next chart, we can see that positive earnings trends become visible in J.P. Morgan's quarterly results during the periods that follow Jamie Dimon's insider buying activity. J.P. Morgan's period of earnings stagnation clearly ends at the beginning of 2016 (which is precisely the time CEO Dimon makes substantial insider stock buys valued at $26 million):

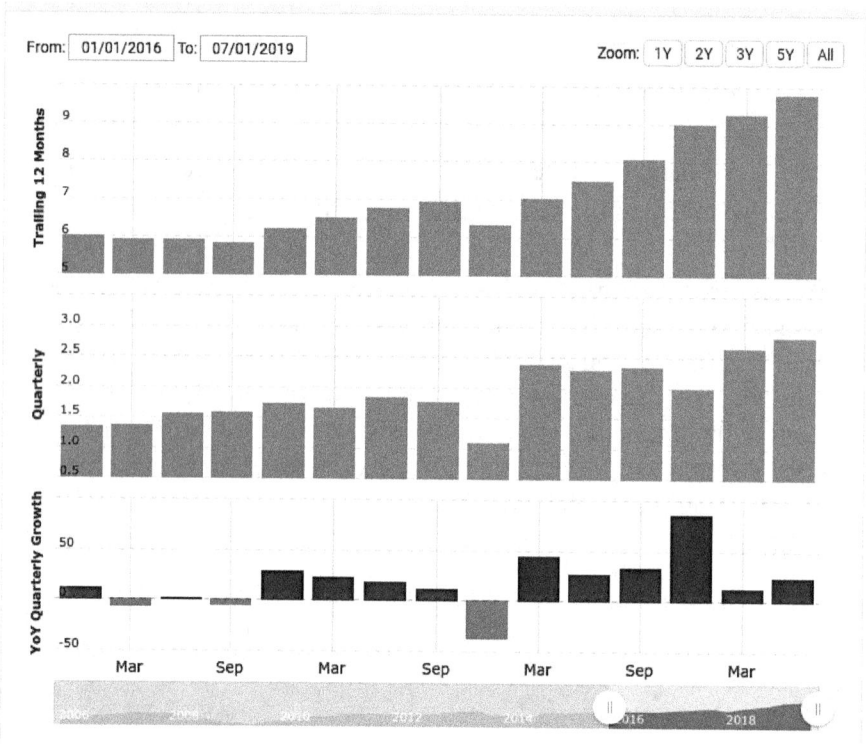

(Source: Macrotrends)

While equities markets experienced growing downside volatility in February of 2016 and a rising number of financial analysts worried about the possibility of a global recession, Jamie Dimon viewed his company's asset performances from the alternative perspective of a corporate insider.

Eventually, Jamie Dimon began calling for investor calm in public commentaries and the J.P. Morgan Chase CEO explained that the broader equities market was trading at inexpensive valuations. Dimon backed up these projections with a contrarian purchase of 500,000 shares of his company's stock at a time when shares of JPM has traded under long-term selling pressure. After he began buying near the 2016 lows, the value of Dimon's stock holdings in JPM surged by almost $230 million in a period of less than one year.

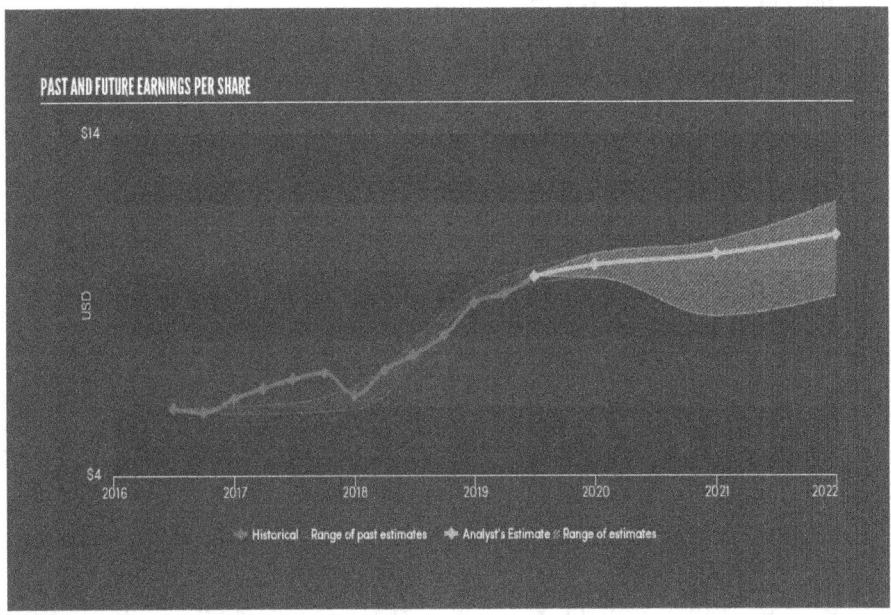

(Source: Simply Wall Street)

Of course, Jamie Dimon never officially called a complete end to the collective stock declines that characterized the 2008 financial crisis, but many commentators have since referred to these events as the Dimon Bottom. In the chart above, we can see these positive earnings projections are likely to continue into 2022 and this should help to support positions for investors with exposure to JPM stock or bonds.

Historical Backtesting Results: Insider-Based Income Strategies

For income investors, the central hypothesis is that legal insider trading activities (both buying and selling decisions) reveal important information that investors can use to assess corporate credit quality and predict future share price performances in publicly traded stocks. Moreover, the long-term trends that are visible in historical backtesting results support the conclusion that profitable investment strategies can be constructed using the SEC's publicly available information on insider trading activity.

When designing a successful insider trading strategy:

- Apply event-based analysis concepts to financial investments and determine suitable buying/selling triggers for individual companies.

Academic Studies: Event-Based Analysis Techniques

In 1997, A. C. MacKinlay introduced a technique called event-based analysis. Following Day 0 (the day of the event), companies impacted by favorable news events experience average future returns that outperform relative to companies that receive no significant news releases.

The opposite scenario also holds true (companies impacted by negative news events experience negative average returns and underperform relative to companies that release no significant news). In the following chart, we can see a visual representation of the trends that mark MacKinlay's findings:

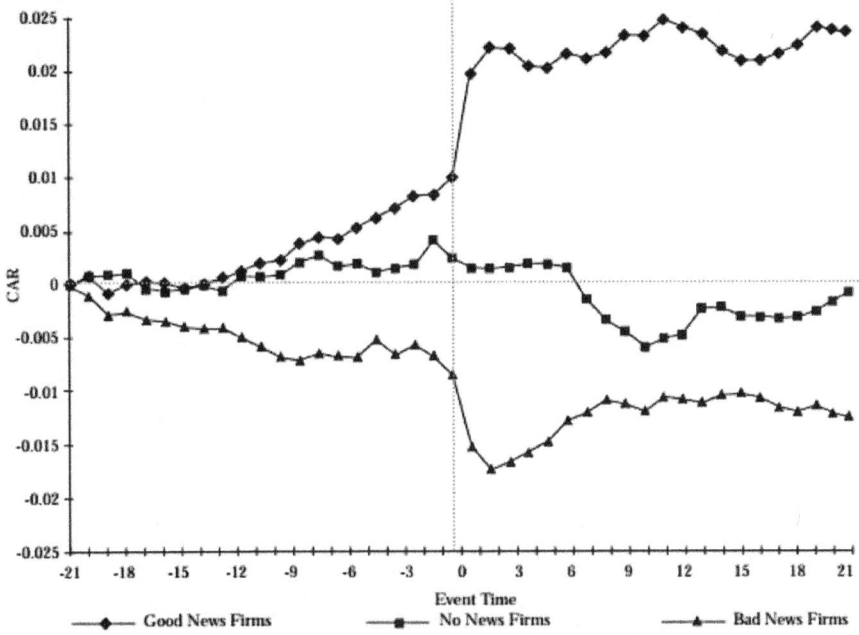

Figure 2a. Plot of cumulative abnormal return for earning announcements from event day -20 to event day 20. The abnormal return is calculated using the market model as the normal return measure.

(Source: Lucena Research)

Conclusion: *Event-based market reactions can be used by investors as a reliable buying or selling signal (depending on the directional nature of the news event).*

Insider Buying/Selling Actions as Momentum Indicators

Extensions of MacKinlay's event-based concepts can be included as a way of analyzing the SEC's insider trading information and used as an event-based source of data. According to research studies conducted by Nejat Seyhun, insider trading actions tend to be characterized by strong momentum that helps drive potential trend direction. When insiders buy stock, the probability for continued purchases the following month is roughly 38%. In contrast, the probability for a reversal in this activity (insiders selling stock) during the following month is just 11%.

Similarly, when insiders are net sellers of stock, the probability for continued sales transactions in the following month is roughly 41%. Probability for a reversal in this activity (insiders buying stock) in the following month is just 10%. This shows us that the odds ratio for new insider transactions that are followed by continued transactions in the same direction (either buying or selling) during the following month is roughly 4:1. However, momentum signals generated by top executives are even stronger (30% probability of continued investment activity the following month vs. 2% probability of reversed direction in transactions) at a ratio of 15:1.

As a result, strong positive correlations between past and future insider investment activities can work as an excellent indicator of market trading momentum trends in the future (in both bullish and bearish directions). This evidence also tells us that when insiders react to special information, market-moving momentum created by their actions can signal buying and selling opportunities for an extended period of time.

Tracking Performances of Insider Trading Decisions

Lucena Research conducted a study based on an aggregation of several statistical inputs used to determine a rating system for companies after significant insider trading activities were reported. In the study, corporate insiders are defined as directors or high-ranking officers of a public company, owning at least 10% of any class of company stock (SEC Act of 1934). Company ratings were based on information gleaned from SEC filings and included these additional factors:

- **Insider transaction sizes** (based on dollar value as well as the total percentage of insider holdings).
- **Number of corporate insiders** following the same course of action (buying or selling).
- **Comparative decision tracking:** If an insider also holds an upper-level position at additional companies, are similar buy/sell decisions being made with respect to those stocks?
- **Trading momentum:** Acceleration/deceleration in the overall trend of a stock's insider activity.
- **Stock price trends:** Market price action visible in the stocks traded by insiders.

Once compiled, these factors were mapped as part of a rating scale which extended from +3 (Extremely Bullish) to -3 (Extremely Bearish):

+3	●●●	Extremely Bullish
+2	●●○	Very Bullish
+1	●○○	Bullish
+0.5	◐○○	Leaning Bullish
+0	○○○	Insignificantly Bullish
0	○○○	Conflicting Purchases & Sales
-0	○○○	Insignificantly Bearish
-0.5	◐○○	Leaning Bearish
-1	●○○	Bearish
-2	●●○	Very Bearish
-3	●●●	Extremely Bearish

(Graphic Source: Lucena Research)

Performance Results: Insider Trading Strategies Consistently Outperform S&P 500 Benchmark

Historical Backtesting –

Strategy-Specific Results Based on Insider Trading Decisions

Backtesting results in Lucena's research study focuses on the positive end of its insider trading ratings spectrum, implementing a long-only position strategy as a way of testing predictive accuracy and the potential for long-term profitability.

An event-based trading strategy was implemented using a full transaction-based simulation, including realistic modeling of transaction costs, using the threshold and holding period defined by the above event study.

The strategy purchases shares of stock in companies with new ratings at 0.5 (or above) and exits positions after a period of 15 days. Stop-loss orders and stop-gain orders are set at +/-5% in order to eliminate positive/negative extremes in the market.

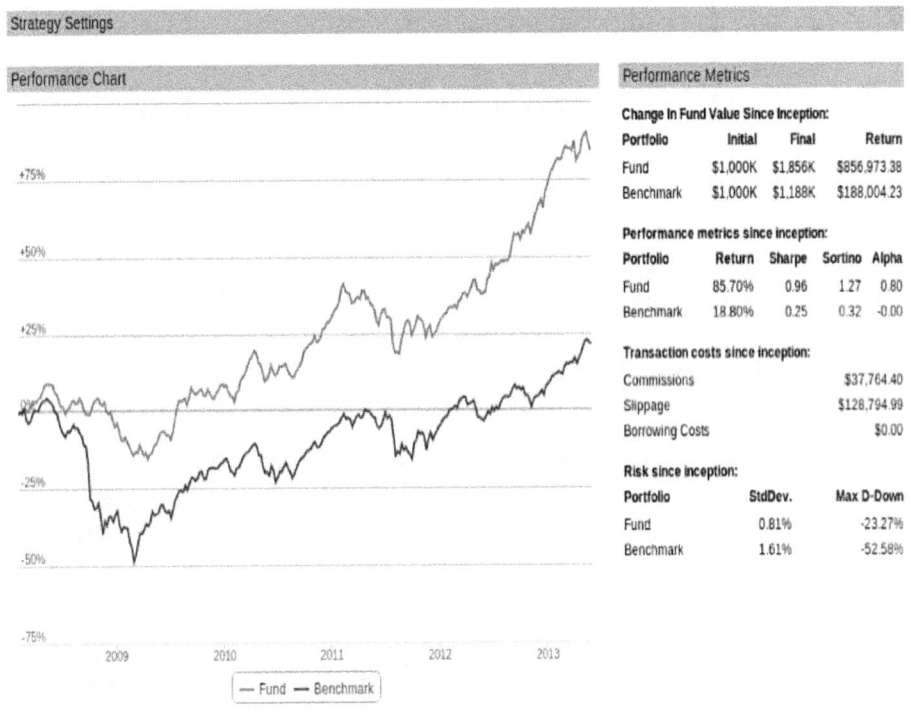

(Source: Lucena Research)

Under the strategy, each event triggers a portfolio allocation of 50% (if less funding is available, the remainder is allocated). If multiple events occur during a single session, the total daily allocation (50%) would be divided evenly amongst all events that day (with a maximum limit of 10 events each day).

Modeling for transaction costs included per-share commissions of $0.0035 per share ($5 minimum) with slippage of five basis points estimated for each transaction. This indicates market prices will move against the portfolio by 0.05% (both entering and exiting each trade).

The performance of this strategy used the S&P 500 as a benchmark, shown in the previous chart. Overall, the study's backtests show highly encouraging results and demonstrate that strategies based on insider buy/sell decisions generate alpha above the broader market, with average annual returns of roughly 14% (even with the presence of slippage and additional transaction costs).

Market Performance Comparisons: Randomized Backtesting

As the control set, the study introduced a series of random tests (10 in total) to determine the existence of potential bias in the data results. Each random test includes the same distribution data from the ratings characterizations used in the initial test, but the data points were randomized within the database. Sample performances generated by the control experiment are shown in the chart below:

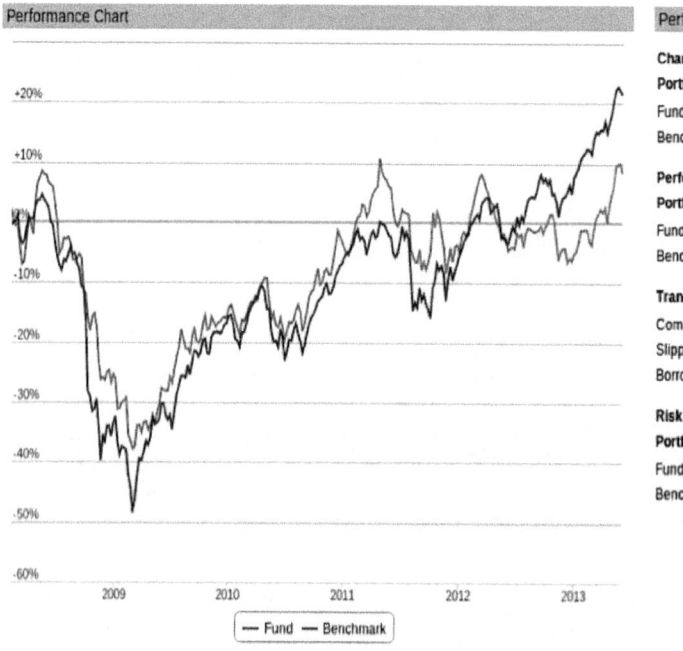

(Source: Lucena Research)

Across ten different control tests, the average total return of 16.35% significantly underperformed the 85.7% average total return generated by the insider-based trading strategy used in the study. The control tests produced an average Sharpe Ratio 0.18, far below the average ratio of 0.96 associated with the insider-based trading strategy.

Conclusion: Weaker performances produced by the control portfolios suggest alpha is present in the market's insider trading data and that investment strategies designed to capitalize on this information can be implemented in a repeatable fashion.

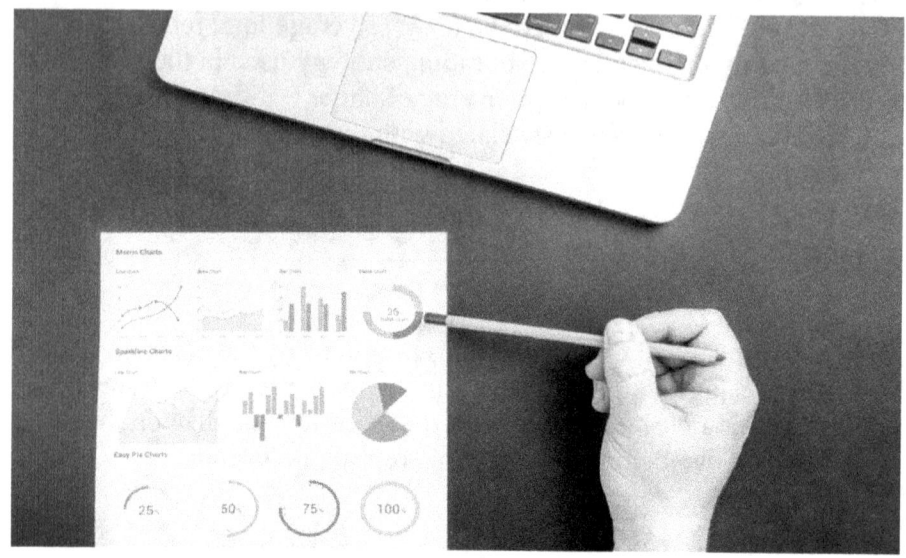

Longer-Term Lessons for Income Investors

The inability of the ratings agencies to release accurate reporting (i.e. the belated nature of 2008 corporate downgrades) should work as a critical lesson for anyone structuring a bond portfolio: Income investors should never rely on ratings agencies for the information that's used to define the credit quality of an investment. Even if we were to assume (for the sake of argument) that the ratings characterizations made by the major agencies are untainted by a clear conflict of interest, it would still be true that the value of their assessments is largely voided by the passage of time.

A classic illustration of the flaws still present in the ratings system can be found in the Enron debacle. For years, the failing energy company falsified large portions of its reported profit totals before declaring bankruptcy in December 2001. However, the major rating agencies failed to downgrade Enron's debt to junk status until four days prior to the collapse of the company. Ultimately, these inexcusable delays led to significant losses for investors with active positions in Enron's stock and bonds.

One reason the performance of the ratings agencies was so poor is that they simply failed to conduct the analysis that would be required to uncover the company's growing problems. In hearings before Congress, one Standard & Poor's analyst covering Enron admitted he hadn't even read several important financial filings released before the company's bankruptcy. However, these wrongdoings extend far beyond basic human error and there is little reason to believe that these past failures are unlikely to happen again in the future.

Other reasons are much more pernicious in nature. In November 2001, Enron learned that Moody's was ready to downgrade its corporate bonds to junk status and the company quickly responded by exerting pressure behind the scenes. Executives at Moody's received phone calls from CEOs at the New York Stock Exchange, J.P. Morgan, and Chevron while former Treasury secretary Robert Rubin reached out to officials at the White House to act on Enron's behalf.

As a result, Moody's delayed its downgrade (and reduced its severity). This allowed Enron's bonds to keep an investment-grade rating despite the massive warning signs that were already visible in the company's underlying operations. Ultimately, income investors should never depend on the major ratings agencies for a timely credit quality analysis of any corporate bond investment. These agencies are almost always the last to know —and that's because they have a vested interest in maintaining the status quo.

Conclusions for Portfolio Strategists

- **Income investors are at risk if they select their portfolio investments based simply on the status quo.**

- **Given the horrendous track record exhibited by the major credit ratings agencies (and lack of a "fix" after the financial crisis), investors must be more proactive in the decision-making processes involved in portfolio construction.**

- **A combined approach that includes credit quality assessments based on common sense balance sheet analysis, short-term bond duration, and buy/sell signals from corporate investors can offer the ability to outperform.**

Broad Perspective: Defining an Income Investment Approach

Given all the highly publicized examples of insider trading decisions, it shouldn't come as much of a surprise that insider trading activity is widely prevalent. Amongst members of upper management (i.e. directors and other corporate executives) this type of trading activity occurs every day in the world's stock markets.

For some investors, what might be most surprising about this activity is that it's fully legal when conducted with the knowledge and sanction of the SEC after submitting the appropriate documents. Most importantly, legal insider data can be an excellent source of strategic ideas for external investors (non-insiders). This is true, no matter what investment style you prefer to use. Furthermore, insider trading activity can be an invaluable indicator when analyzing stocks that are already included in your portfolio.

Overall, case examples from companies like Twitter, Square, General Electric, and J.P. Morgan Chase show us that insider trading information can be particularly valuable when assessing the credit quality of a company, the strength of its bond offerings, and the likely trajectory of stock performances after these buy/sell decisions are made.

After all, is anyone in a better position to know a company's credit profile better its own management team? Top executives can hardly be expected to forget relevant points that might have emerged from the company's last sales report or the information that was discussed in recent strategy meetings. As a result, corporate insiders will obviously have access to materially important, non-public information that can be used to guide new investment decisions.

Remember, this doesn't involve the same types of illegal trading decisions made by people like Ivan Boesky (who relied on a network of informants to secure profits on his positions). Instead, the insider trading decisions described here are those made by managerial directors and other corporate executives when buying or selling shares of their own companies. This insider trading activity is fully legal because corporate executives report their trading decisions to the SEC via "Form 4" documentation. When investors analyze the Form 4s that have been filed at the SEC, it's possible to follow along with the investment decisions made by people that are truly in the know.

Historical backtesting results show that this approach to data analysis can be favorable in generating superior returns in long-term portfolio investments. As further evidence of this phenomenon, it should be noted that for many years institutional investors have successfully used insider trading data from the SEC as a way of guiding their own investment decisions. The central hypothesis is that an analysis of legal insider stock trades (whether they involve selling shares or buying shares), can reveal important information about a company's true credit quality. Ultimately, this allows investors to more accurately predict the strength of its future earnings performances.

If this hypothesis is true, its implications support the conclusion that profitable trading strategies can be constructed using SEC information on a company's recent insider trading activity. In other words, this form of directed event-based analysis can be used to determine purchasing triggers that are suitable for selecting investments in stocks and corporate bonds.

According to research conducted by Victor Niederhoffer and J. H. Lorie (University of Chicago, 1968), insider trading activity (and the accumulation of insider buying actions, in particular) can have a persistent impact on the share price of a company's stock for up to six months into the future. As a result of their studies, Lorie and Niederhoffer concluded that proper analysis of insider trading data can lead to profitable investment decisions and that the SEC should provide faster dissemination of these statistics in order to give investors a more actionable source of information when making relevant stock selections.

Core Income Investment Strategies

When constructing strategies for income portfolios, we have seen that historical results strongly suggest insider buying signals tend to generate market returns that are superior when compared to the traditional valuation metrics often used in passive index investing. For these reasons, portfolio strategists should consider the following list of factors when designing an approach to corporate bond selection in the current economic environment:

- Historical backtesting data show that investments guided by insider activities can generate returns that are significantly higher than the returns generated by passive index funds.
- Additionally, insider trading activities are more informative than most of the popular valuation metrics (such as the price-earnings ratio, dividend yield, or book-to-market ratio).
- Insider trading activities have interactive effects which influence these commonly used metrics.
- Understanding the trends visible in insider buying/selling activities can change the interpretation of a book-to-market ratio or a price-to-earnings ratio.

Comparing Traditional Portfolio Investment Strategies

- **Value-Based Investment Approach**

Value-based investments use the price-earnings ratio (P/E) or book-to-market ratio (B/M) to uncover opportunities in companies that are undervalued and capable of generating above-average returns in the future. A value-based approach will generally focus on companies exhibiting a low P/E ratio or a high B/M ratio under the expectation that markets will eventually raise valuation levels to match the company's favorable earnings results or higher book asset values.

- **Growth-Based Investment Approach**

Growth-based techniques aim to identify companies with price momentum and/or earnings momentum. Buying assets tied to companies with rising earnings growth or recent rallies in share prices is a strategy that enables investors to capitalize on the company's underlying momentum characteristics. Growth-based approaches focus on companies with high price-to-earnings ratios and low book-to-market ratios. Using this strategy, portfolio managers will often compare a company's earnings growth rate with its P/E to help ensure that an investment is not over-priced.

As one notable example of this approach, Peter Lynch (former manager of the Magellan Fund) became well-known for selecting companies with a high B/M ratio or an earnings growth rate that is higher than its P/E ratio. Generally speaking, growth investment strategies tend to accept greater risk levels in exchange for the opportunity to gain exposure to a company's underlying market momentum (based on the potential for rapid expansion in earnings).

Overcoming Problems Using Traditional Valuation Metrics in Isolation

Traditional valuation metrics (in and of themselves) are unable to distinguish between a profitable investment opportunity and a situation where low share prices simply compensate for additional risk exposure.

In contrast, insider trading activities contain independent value indicators that are forward-looking in nature. Defined by the number of shares bought or sold, insider trading decisions are based on expectations of future developments that are not necessarily dependent on current share prices. As each investment transaction is planned, corporate insiders utilize their knowledge of emerging developments within the company, its industry, and the broader economy.

Correct assessments are rewarded with profits, whereas incorrect assessments are punished with losses. Traditional valuation metrics lack the wealth consequences that are associated with these types of insider trading decisions. Thus, investment signals contained in P/E ratios, B/M ratios, dividend yield, and earnings growth rates can be augmented (strengthened) by insider trading actions that support the prevailing outlook (either bullish or bearish). In other words, corroborating signals from both approaches can be combined to increase the chances of success in developing a sustainably profitable portfolio strategy.

Assessing Validity/Strength of Insider Trading Signals

- **Selecting Favorable Insider Signals**

Why not simply read the publicly available information and follow all of the buy/sell actions of corporate insiders?

To compile all relevant information, hundreds of thousands of insider stock purchases and sales each year must be added to the even larger number of private transactions, exercises of stock options, and other types of stock acquisitions/dispositions. As a result, smaller investors cannot cope with the sheer volume of insider trading information that is publicly available.

Instead, investors need proven strategies which focus on a subset of well-guided insider transactions that are likely to generate enhanced returns for a portfolio.

- Insider purchases indicate good news (relative to insiders' sales).
- The actions of CEOs Jack Dorsey and Jamie Dimon work as comprehensive examples of how these trends actually operate in the market.
- Income portfolio strategies can benefit from an early analysis of trends in buying or selling activities initiated by top-level corporate insiders.

Combining Income Investment Strategies

How do insider trading signals work in conjunction with these traditional strategies?

Metrics like dividend yield, P/E ratio, and B/M ratio are constructed using current stock prices. Since all of this information is already reflected in the market price, these metrics are backward-looking in nature.

When a stock's price declines, its P/E ratio drops while its B/M ratio and dividend yield move higher. This could signal a buying opportunity (and greater future returns) if the company becomes undervalued relative to its peers.

At the same time, it should be understood that if falling share prices are reflective of underlying problems within the company, traditional valuation signals are simply picking up an additional risk premium (rather than a sustainable opportunity for profits).

Overcoming Current Challenges in Corporate Bond Markets

Income portfolios structured with a preference for bonds with shorter duration (average maturities of four years or less) allow investors to avoid risks associated with unanticipated changes in the long-term interest rate outlook. Thus, fixed-income investors with fund holdings that track the aggregate bond index should consider balancing these positions with shorter-term investments.

In this way, investors can lower the average duration present in fixed-income portfolio holdings and identify assets that are better suited to meet expected risk tolerance levels. Holding bonds with a shorter duration can also create benefits when they provide additional liquidity for short-term needs.

Innovative strategies that combine favorable bond duration parameters with insider buying signals as a proactive component have been shown to produce significant advantages for income investors. In 2018, many bond funds reported flat (or negative) returns while a select minority of funds implementing a combined strategic approach have bucked the trend and generated impressive returns.

For income investors, this creates the potential for problems that exist on several different fronts. As the major ratings agencies continue to mischaracterize the strength of corporate bond investments, trends in the market's average credit quality continue to deteriorate and the underlying trajectory in global interest rates has grown increasingly uncertain.

In this challenging market environment, income investors must implement protective strategies capable of achieving enhanced returns that are sustainable over the long-term.

When fixed-income investors monitor insider trading as an approach to identify assets backed by above-average credit quality, they can achieve targeted asset diversification that is positioned to outperform the common bond benchmarks. Moreover, this approach can work as an excellent strategy to avoid potential surprises, as well as ensuring a given investment outlook matches expectations for risk tolerance.

Designing a Sustainable Approach to Selecting Income Portfolio Investments

- Focus on companies with a rock-solid balance sheet with collateral that is sufficient to back all corporate bond investments.
- For example, Twitter has $5.9 billion in cash and short-term securities vs $3.3 billion in total debt (thus, Twitter can pay down all debt today). 4.2% yield to maturity for their bonds is quite compelling (despite its relatively weak corporate bond rating).
- Examine flaws with traditional ratings analysis and challenges that exist in the current market environment (reasons many funds have underperformed).
- Provide investors with a proactive strategy that is multi-faceted and capable of outperforming the traditional approach to income investing.

- Income investment strategies based on publicly available insider trading information (made available by the SEC) can work as a confirmatory analytical component when making bond portfolio selections.

Long-Term Strategies to Structure Income Portfolios

In many cases, income investment strategies are designed to track the performance of a common bond benchmark. However, this approach tends to create added risk exposure that is beyond the expected tolerance levels of most investors.

Recent trends in the aggregate bond index show that many bond funds are structured around maturities above seven years while trends in corporate bond markets show average maturities that are even longer in duration. Overall, these extended averages expose income investors to the negative influences often encountered during uncertain interest rate environments.

When elevated credit risks are combined with an uncertain interest rate environment, the result is often relative underperformance in returns when compared to what is seen in the broader market. Ultimately, short-duration bond funds tend to perform better in these types of challenging rate environments. Bond benchmarks can work as a productive guideline when developing an effective approach to fixed-income strategy.

However, these instruments shouldn't necessarily dictate the specific investment decisions that are involved when constructing an active portfolio. Instead, a targeted focus on insider trading signals can make it easier for investors to identify well-positioned bonds backed by strong credit quality and a sustainably positive outlook for future earnings. With this sustainable approach, investors are able to diversify income portfolios away from the inadequate components that are generally present in common benchmark indexes.

Strategic Summary –

Income Investor Keys to Success

- **Identify compelling buy signals from top-level corporate insiders**

- **Find firms with a fortress balance sheet confirmed by strong debt/equity metrics**

- **Focus on bonds with short maturity to avoid uncertainties connected to unpredictable interest rate environments**

www.ingramcontent.com/pod-product-compliance
Lightning Source LLC
Chambersburg PA
CBHW060847220526
45466CB00003B/1276